THE SAILOR'S WORLD

The David & Charles Series

THE SAILOR'S WORLD

CAPTAIN T. A. HAMPTON
AFC, C Eng, MRINA

Illustrations by John Horsley

UNABRIDGED

PAN BOOKS LTD : LONDON

First published 1968 by David & Charles (Publishers) Ltd.
This edition published 1971 by Pan Books Ltd,
33 Tothill Street, London, S.W.1

I S B N 0 330 02683 6

*Printed and bound in England by
Hazell Watson & Viney Ltd, Aylesbury, Bucks*

CONTENTS

ILLUSTRATIONS IN PHOTOGRAVURE

(between pages 80 and 81)

Aerial view of the Port of London below Tower Bridge
(Copyright of the Port of London Authority)

The motor-ship *Niso*, of 119,378 tons
(By courtesy of Shell International Marine Ltd)

The 58,000-ton Cunard liner, *Queen Elizabeth II*
(By courtesy of John Brown & Co (Clydebank) Ltd)

The offshore drilling rig *Sea Quest*
(By courtesy of Harland & Wolff Ltd)

SRN 6 Hovercraft

The gaff-rigged ketch *Harebell*
(By courtesy of Beken & Sons Ltd)

The Sail Training Association's three-masted schooner
Sir Winston Churchill

An R N L I fast inshore-rescue boat
(R N L I copyright)

A new type of 44-ft steel lifeboat now in service
with the R N L I
(R N L I copyright)

CHAPTER ONE

Around The Headlands

LIGHTHOUSES

Many of our famous headlands proudly wear the snow-white structure of a lighthouse, with its attendant cottages and workshops. Although of less importance to the modern navigator with his radar, it still offers the final check on other methods of position-finding at sea.

The distance at which a light may be seen from out at sea is limited by the curvature of the earth, rather than the power of the light. The higher the light and the shipborne observer, the farther round the curve of the earth will the light be seen.

The highest lighthouse in the British Isles is at Barra Head on the west coast of Scotland, 620 feet above sea level. The light itself is mounted in a sixty-foot tower and, in clear weather, can be seen from thirty-three miles out at sea. Another high lighthouse is the South Foreland, situated on a cliff 374 feet above sea level. One disadvantage of being so high is that the light is sometimes obscured by low cloud,

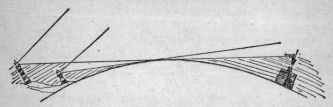

The seaman can ascertain his distance from a lighthouse by observing it just as it appears over the horizon

though visibility at sea level may be quite good. The average visibility of our principal lighthouses is approximately twenty miles.

The friendly lighthouse not only provides the seaman with direction, but will also tell him his distance off if he observes it just as it appears over the horizon. At night, especially when there is cloud in the sky, the reflection of the light – which we call the 'loom' – can be seen long before the actual light, so the navigator is ready to note the instant the light appears or 'dips'. He can then find out how far he is away from the lighthouse by reference to a set of tables known as 'Distance Off Lights'.

The 'distance off' can also be found by measuring with a sextant the angle the lantern makes with the horizontal and, by taking compass bearings of the lighthouse, the navigator's own actual position can then be ascertained.

The lighthouse is, perhaps, man's earliest aid to safe navigation. Priests in 700 BC maintained fires on top of towers in Lower Egypt, and it is known that a lighthouse existed on Cape Incihisari at this time. The best-known lighthouse of those early days was built on the island of Pharos, near Alexandria, by Sostratus of Cnidus, during the third century. It was about 500 feet high, and is said to have been visible for thirty miles out to sea.

Britain's first lighthouse was built by the Romans at Dover Castle, and present-day visitors can still see the original Roman workmanship. An early coal-fire tower, on the island of St Agnes, in the Scilly Isles, was fitted with a lantern in 1680, and although no longer in use, the original lantern still remains.

The first lighthouses used wood fires as the source of illumination. After 1500, coal fires or candles were used in the majority of lighthouses until about 1780, when the advantages of parabolic reflectors combined with oil lamps became better understood. Next came the development of Argand's burner, followed at the beginning of the nineteenth century by multiple-wick oil burners, as many as ten concentric wicks being in use in major lighthouses. By the end of the nineteenth century, the first vaporized oil burners with incandescent mantles were in use, and an improved version of this type is still used in isolated rock and island lighthouses.

Electricity came to the fore in 1922 with the development of a satisfactory high-power electric filament lamp, although as far back as 1862 electricity had been tried experimentally in some lighthouses. Today most major lighthouses employ electric filament lamps, and vaporized burners are gradually disappearing as major modernization schemes are completed. In some minor unwatched lighthouses, dissolved acetylene gas is still being used, the gas being stored in cylinders.

A light that could not be identified would have a very limited value to the seaman, so the lens panels through which the light is focused are designed to rotate to produce identifying flashes. The light at Souter Point, for example, makes four revolutions per minute, and shows a flashing red light of 1,380,000 candlepower every five seconds. If the duration of the light is shorter than the dark period, it is termed a flashing light, but if the dark period is the lesser it is said to be an occulting light. If dark and light periods are of equal duration, it is termed 'isophase'.

The characteristics of navigational lights are shown on mariner's charts in the following terms: ie, Fixed (F); Group Flashing (Gp.F.); Group Occulting (Gp.O.); Fixed Flashing and Fixed Group Flashing (F.Fl.) and (F.Gp.Fl.); Quick Flashing (Qk.Fl.) and Alternating (Alt.).

SOUND SIGNALS

In addition to the light, most lighthouses emit an audible warning to the mariner during conditions of low visibility. These sound signals can be made by explosives, compressed air, electrically-vibrated diaphragms, electric fog signals and, occasionally, by bells, but the range of the latter is limited.

The explosive sound signal is made by detonating a four-ounce charge suspended from a jib, and fired electrically. Such signals have a range of about four miles, but their use is limited as it involves continual reloading by the lighthouse crew. A smaller explosive fog signal is the Moyes acetylene fog gun, which will fire shots continuously without attention, but it has a range of only one mile and is no longer used in the Trinity House Service, the authority responsible for our lightships and lighthouses.

Compressed air apparatus is the most common fog signal device around the British Isles, and there are three different types. Of these, the reed emits a high-pitched note of around 500 vibrations per second (C in the treble clef), but as it can only pass a small quantity of air, its range is little more than two miles under good conditions and it is used for secondary or minor lighthouses. The siren and the diaphone, on the other hand, can be designed to take over forty-five cubic feet of air a second, and they represent the major fog signals in the British Isles. The siren is a rotating instrument and the diaphone has a piston with a reciprocating motion. Both produce low but very powerful notes of approximately 150 vibrations per second (C to F in the bass clef). The diaphone has a distinctive grunt at the end of its note. Special fog marks are laid down for each lighthouse station if possible and when these cease to be visible the fog signal is operated.

During daylight hours, mainland lighthouse structures and those on high rocky islands, provide an excellent 'day mark' in the shape of a white beacon. However, when the structure is not on the skyline, but has a background of rock or white cliff, the tower may be painted with bands of colour to make it more conspicuous, or even all black so that it stands out in relief against white cliffs.

WIND AND VISIBILITY SCALES

Beaufort Number	Wind speed in knots	Description of wind	
0	Less than 1	Calm	—
1	1 to 3	Light Air	Yachts have steerage way with wind free
2	4 to 6	Light Breeze	Yachts can carry light-weather sails
3	7 to 10	Gentle Breeze	Yachts begin to heel over
4	11 to 15	Moderate Breeze	Good working breeze Yachts heel well over
5	16 to 20	Fresh Breeze	Yachts reef down
6	21 to 26	Strong Breeze	Yachts reef right down
7	27 to 33	Moderate Gale	Yachts remain in harbour or 'heave to' at sea
8	34 to 40	Fresh Gale	—
9	41 to 47	Strong Gale	—
10	48 to 55	Whole Gale	—
11	56 to 65	Storm	—
12	Above 65	Hurricane	—

FOG AND VISIBILITY SCALE

0	Dense Fog	Objects not visible at 50 yards
1	Thick Fog	,, ,, ,, ,, 1 cable (1/10 mile)
2	Fog	,, ,, ,, ,, 2 cables
3	Moderate Fog	,, ,, ,, ,, ½ mile
4	Mist or Haze Very Poor Visibility	,, ,, ,, ,, 1 mile
5	Poor Visibility	,, ,, ,, ,, 2 miles
6	Moderate Visibility	,, ,, ,, ,, 5 miles
7	Good Visibility	,, ,, ,, ,, 10 miles
8	Very Good Visibility	,, ,, ,, ,, 30 miles
9	Excellent Visibility	,, ,, ,, ,, more than 30 miles

At sea, the force of the wind and the distance visible are both measured by numerical notations which are internationally recognized. The notation for indicating wind force, known as the Beaufort Scale after the British admiral who devised it, and the Fog and Visibility Scale, are shown on the previous page.

A typical coastguard station and signal mast

THE COASTGUARD SERVICE

HM Coastguard Stations are, like lighthouses, also situated on high ground around our coast, the older ones often being identifiable by a row of white cottages. Many of these cottages are now in private hands, the coastguard watch-keeping service being maintained from less attractive, but more efficient premises.

At coastguard stations, as well as at lighthouse establishments, the most prominent feature is probably the mast from which storm signals are flown for the benefit of seafarers. When a gale is expected within twelve hours, or is actually in progress, a cone, three feet high and three feet wide at the base, is hoisted by signal halyards up the mast. If the gale is expected to blow from the south, the point of the cone is downwards, and if from the north, upwards. These day signals are flown until dusk and replaced during the hours of darkness by three lights, usually red, forming a similar cone.

The coastguard service is a coast-watching organization whose primary function today is life-saving. There is a regular force of more than 500 uniformed coastguardsmen assisted by nearly 7,000 auxiliaries, who are attached to some 400 stations and look-out posts situated in commanding positions

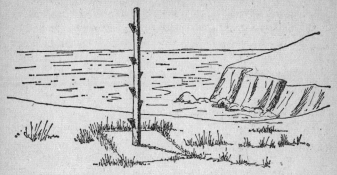

A cliff-side 'monkey' post for use in coastguard rescue operations

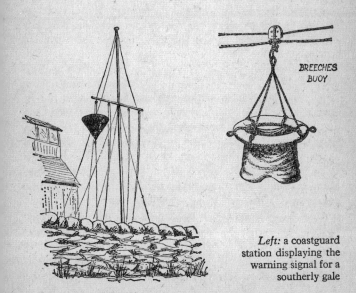

BREECHES BUOY

Left: a coastguard station displaying the warning signal for a southerly gale

round the coasts of Great Britain and Northern Ireland. These stations are equipped with rocket life-saving apparatus and local teams of volunteers are available to man this equipment in an emergency.

If it is necessary to get the crew of a stranded ship ashore, through heavy surf, when the landing of a boat is impossible, a rocket is fired across the stricken vessel, carrying a light line up to 450 yards long. The crew then haul out a block (pulley) and endless whip (line) from the shore, and make it fast high up in the ship's structure. A heavy rope is then hauled out to the wreck on the endless whip, and the end secured three feet higher than the block. Ashore, a travelling block is fitted to the higher rope, or 'jackstay', and the whip and a breeches buoy are secured to it and hauled out to the wreck by means of the endless line. One man at a time gets into the breeches buoy, facing shorewards, and is hauled to safety by the rescue team.

On cliff sides, or other conveniently high positions, a 'monkey' post will sometimes be found erected to serve as an anchorage for the endless whip and the jackstay, and to facilitate training in rescue operations. With convenient footholds, they make excellent observation poles.

LLOYD'S SIGNAL STATIONS

In strategic locations around our coasts, usually on headlands, there are maritime signalling stations which are manned both day and night by staff members of the Corporation of Lloyd's. They handle commercial shipping intelligence between owners and shipmasters, and communicate by means of International Code flags and morse lamp. In the past, mechanical semaphore machines were more often used, and these may still be seen on occasions, but today semaphore signalling is mainly carried out by a signalman holding orange- and red-diagonal flags.

COMMERCIAL MARITIME SIGNAL STATIONS

The following are some of the signal stations in the British Isles at which signals are received from and made to merchant vessels of all nations.

SOUTH COAST	EAST COAST
Deal	North Shields
Fort Gilkicker (Spithead)	Bridlington
Berry Head (Brixham)	Gorleston
Falmouth	Southend
The Lizard	Margate

WEST COAST

St Ives	St Ann's Head
Hartland Point	Fishguard
Barry Island	Holyhead
The Mumbles	Ramsey (Isle of Man)

MARTELLO TOWERS

These round granite towers, sometimes with a ditch around them, can be seen here and there along the southern and eastern coasts of Britain. They were built in large numbers as a defence against possible invasion during the Napoleonic Wars. Each tower provided an elevated gun platform and accommodation for the small garrison. The only access was through an entrance some twenty feet above the ground, reached by means of a retractable ladder. Their name derives from Cape Martello in Corsica, where a tower of this kind was unsuccessfully attacked by a landing-party.

DAY MARKS

Some harbour entrances are difficult to locate when making an approach from seawards, being hidden amongst the folds of hills and cliffs. At night, an identifying light at the entrance

solves the problem, but by day the mariner, perhaps visiting
the port for the first time, does not have this advantage. Dartmouth, in south Devon, is a case in point, and a truncated
pyramid, built of granite, stands on the cliff top to the east of
the entrance 500 feet above sea level. Eighty feet high and
most conspicuous, it provides a guide whilst the entrance itself
is still way down below the horizon.

These marks, together with other navigational aids, are
listed for the seaman in Admiralty publications known as
Pilots. Channel Pilot, Part 1, covers the area from the Scilly
Isles and the south coast of England from Pendeen Point to
Foreness. These sailing directions can be obtained from Ad-
miralty chart agents and are the sailor's navigational 'bibles'.

PROHIBITED ANCHORAGE BEACONS

When a submarine cable is laid on the sea bed offshore it is
reasonably safe from damage by shipping as a vessel is unlikely to anchor in deep water, but inshore, and in harbours,
the risk of damage is great. These areas are, therefore, clearly
marked on the seaman's charts, and beacons carrying a red and
white diamond shape are erected on high ground
ashore, probably bearing the words 'Telegraph
Cable'.

PROHIBITED
ANCHORAGE

There may be one beacon low down on the beach
and another high on the cliff top, behind the lower
one. These two beacons, kept in line, form what the
seaman calls a 'transit', warning him of the line of
the prohibited anchorage.

ANEMOMETERS

Associated with coastguard stations, lighthouse establishments, and also with harbours, ships and airfields, are wind-
driven instruments turning slowly or furiously, depending on
the weather. This apparatus is the Robinson cup-anemometer
which revolves as a result of the wind exerting more pressure
on the open end of the cup than the convex end. Speed of rota-

tion is recorded on a dial, as wind speed, in miles per hour or knots.

Another type which may be seen is the Dines anemometer. This consists mainly of a pressure-head tube, which is kept facing into the wind by a vane on the weathercock principle. The wind pressure varies the level at which the closed chamber, to which it is connected, floats in a container of water. Increase of pressure lifts the chamber, which is connected to a stylograph that records the wind speed on a revolving drum.

CUP ANEMOMETER

CHAPTER TWO

On The Beaches

On the beaches, especially those from which inshore fishing-boats operate, contact with the sea becomes more intimate. The launching and hauling out of boats of around twenty feet in length is a regular chore of the longshoreman, as it has been since man discarded the wicker coracle.

CAPSTANS

One of the oldest devices used for hauling out boats is the capstan. Familiar to us all in illustrations, but not often seen ashore these days, it consists of a round drum, turning on a vertical axle, and anchored securely to the ground. The top of the drum has holes into which wooden bars are inserted, the leverage of the bar providing the mechanical advantage.

With the hauling line secure to the boat, and two or three turns round the drum to take the strain, all spare hands heave

One of the oldest devices for hauling out boats – the capstan

away, someone taking the line off the drum as the boat is
dragged slowly up the beach. To prevent the keel digging into
soft sand, holly staves or other hardwood battens are slipped
under the stem as fast as they are recovered from under the
keel aft, thus providing a primitive but efficient slipway. On
the beaches and in little coves around Britain, lacking the
shelter of a harbour wall, beach launching has been going on
for centuries, and there is a particularly nice example of a
capstan on the beach at Porthgwarra, near Land's End.

TRAINING WALLS

Often on open beaches, or up inlets and creeks, low walls of
stone, concrete, or wood, have been built – apparently for no
reason at all. Their use may not be obvious, but these structures, in fact, do a valuable job in diverting and controlling
tidal streams, preventing sandbanks from building up and
keeping channels open for navigation.

Groynes check erosion and prevent unwanted 'build ups'

GROYNES

Sometimes called jetties, groynes are similar structures which
have been built more or less at right-angles to the shore down
pebble or sand beaches. They are designed to reduce erosion

and to prevent 'build up' of sand or shingle in the wrong places. Wooden, weathered groynes are accepted as part of the seascape, as, too, are the ugly but functional outfalls.

OUTFALLS

Small outfalls are sometimes merely drains, and may not be objectionable, but most large towns on the coast dispose of their sewage out at sea by means of outfall pipes made of concrete or iron, which may be several feet in diameter. At high water they are often unseen, being buried under sand or concrete slabs, but at low water they are likely to be exposed, as

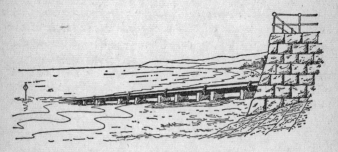

The seaward end of an outfall is usually marked by a beacon

the outlet has to be clear of the bottom to prevent silting up. The seaward end is usually marked by a beacon, to warn shipping of a danger to navigation. The effluent can also be a danger to health, and it is advisable to give them a wide berth when swimming.

PIERS

These may be structures of iron, concrete or timber that extend out to sea from the shore to facilitate the embarkation and landing of passengers where no harbour exists. They also provide the unique sensation of being out at sea without being on a boat. Having a maritime atmosphere all of their own, they de-

light the visitor from way inland, as he fills his lungs with sea air.

The first promenade pier in England was the old chain pier at Brighton. It was built in 1822–3 on a foundation of oak piles, extended 1,136 feet out to sea, and survived for seventy-four years before being destroyed during a gale in 1896.

Two of the longest piers in the British Isles are those at Southend and Southport, both of which have been built out over long, flat beaches. Southend pier is one and a quarter miles long, and the one at Southport is nearly a mile in length.

INSHORE FISHING GEAR

Hanging over walls, on rails or lying on the beach can be seen the working tools of the inshore fisherman – lobster pots, longlines, nets and all the gear that goes with them.

The seine net is a single-mesh net that hangs like a wall in the water. The net has more fullness in the middle than at the ends, and hangs from a cork-buoyed headrope down to a bottom line parallel with it and weighted down by leads. A light

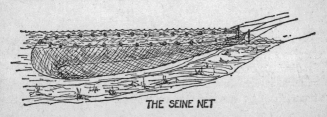

THE SEINE NET

spar at each end keeps the lines apart, and hauling lines are secured by bridles to each spar. The extra amount of net in the middle forms a bag to contain the catch.

When the seine net is used from the shore, a rowing boat or dinghy is needed to take one end out to sea, uncoiling the net as it goes and bringing the end ashore again farther up the beach. Keeping the bottom line tauter than the top one, both are then hauled in evenly until the bag of the net is drawn up the beach, clear of the water.

When used from fishing-boats in deep water, one end of the net can be buoyed as the boat steams round in a circle. Only surface fish are caught but, with deep-sea fishing-boats and their large nets, they are caught in their thousands.

A similar net, but known as a 'drift' net, is used by the Cornish pilchard fishermen. They work at night, a 'dan' buoy with a light on it marking the windward end of their mile-long nets. The fish are caught by their gills as they try to swim through the mesh of the net, and have to be shaken out into baskets as the seemingly endless net is hauled slowly aboard.

TRAWLS

These are conical, bag-shaped nets used for bottom fishing or trawling. They catch mainly flat fish, such as plaice, sole, skate, etc.

The net is towed along the bottom by boats, the net mouth being kept open by means of a beam, or more often nowadays by 'otter' boards. The small conical end of the net, known as the 'bunt' or 'cod' end, can be opened so that the catch may conveniently be spilled out on deck.

The beam of a beam trawl can be identified by the oval-

THE BEAM TRAWL

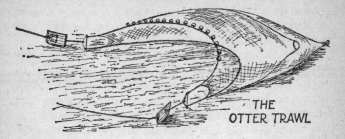

THE
OTTER TRAWL

shaped irons at each end which hold the beam off the bottom and support the headrope of the net. The ground rope, being longer than the headrope, forms a curve or 'bight' behind the beam. As the fish are disturbed, escape upwards is denied them by the net overhead.

The more modern otter trawl is similar in action, but here the mouth of the net is kept open by two 'otter boards' which act as vanes. They are so designed and secured to the net that the pull of the trawl rope or wire gives them a 'sheer' or slant outwards. As the bottom or belly of the net drags along the bottom and suffers most from wear, it is made from coarser twine. The ground rope is weighted with lead or old chain and served round with old rope to about three inches in diameter.

Bottom-feeding fish lie with their heads upstream, so it is best to tow the trawl downstream. Most bottom fish, sensing the approach of the ground line and net, strike forward and downward to bury themselves in the sand. Feeling the net underneath them they try again, but soon find themselves trapped in the small 'cod' end. Soles, however, being more cunning and stronger than other flat fish, will often work their way back along the net and escape. Pockets of net are, therefore, worked into the sides of the main net, so that just when fish think they are winning clear, they find themselves finally cornered.

TRAMMELS

A trammel net is another wall of net but, unlike the seine net, it fishes from the bottom. Its name probably derives from *trois mailles* or three mesh, as it consists of a slack, fine-mesh net walled in by two coarser nets of a mesh large enough for big fish to push through.

The bottom line is weighted with leads to keep it on the bottom and the headrope is buoyed with corks so that it hangs like a curtain. The net is usually 120 fathoms long (six feet to the fathom) and is set overnight, up and down with the current. When anything tries to move through, it pushes the slack fine-mesh net through a mesh of the large outer net, thus forming a bag around itself from which it is impossible to escape. In fact, the difficulty is in removing your catch when you have got it.

LOBSTER POTS

Pots made in the traditional manner with woven withies – branches of the willow or osier – are still used in Devon and in a number of other places around our coasts. However, they are difficult and expensive to make, as well as being awkward to stow in a boat, and are rapidly being replaced by pots made of more modern materials. Some are made of wire netting on wooden frames, some of heavy fish-net on wooden hoops, and some of wooden slats. The very latest ones are made of metal and nylon netting, and collapse for easy storage.

The pattern of lobster pots varies from one locality to another, but they are all based on the one-way system, it being easier to get in than to get out. Fish bait is secured well inside the pot as a lure, and the pots are hauled once or twice a day. Similar pots are used for lobsters and crabs. Once in the pot, the catch is the property of the fisherman – don't rob him, for the life of an inshore fisherman is far from easy.

CHAPTER THREE

Estuaries

At intervals around our coasts are the estuaries of large and small rivers and the mouths of streams that find their way to the sea. The larger ones provide natural harbours for shipping, while the smaller streams and creeks provide shelter for the inshore fisherman and the yachtsman.

It is in the estuaries that we first become conscious of the navigational buoys that guide shipping through deep-water channels, and warn shipmasters of dangerous sandbanks, rocks and wrecks.

NAVIGATIONAL BUOYS

All buoys used for purposes of navigation are in one of three main shapes: conical, can (flat top) or spherical.

When a vessel is travelling in the direction of the flood stream, that is, up river, all conical-shaped buoys must be to starboard (ship's right-hand side), and all can-shaped buoys to port (ship's left-hand side). Spherical buoys can be left to either side. This system is known as the lateral system of buoyage as opposed to the cardinal system, in which buoys are placed in relation to the four cardinal points of the compass.

Buoys in a channel may be numbered or lettered from sea-wards. If they are numbered, odd numbers will be on the starboard side and even numbers on the port side. When travelling in the direction of the ebb stream, down river, colours and numbers will, of course, be reversed.

Starboard-hand buoys are painted black, or in black and white chequers, and port-hand buoys are painted red, or in red and white chequers. Sometimes navigational buoys carry

THE BUOYAGE SYSTEM

CHANNEL MARKER

RED

CHANNEL MARKER

BLACK

CHANNEL MARKER

DIRECTION OF FLOOD TIDE

PASS EITHER SIDE

RED & WHITE

CHANNEL MARKER

BLACK & WHITE

CHANNEL MARKER

WHITE RED

INNER MIDDLE GROUND

WHITE RED

INNER MIDDLE GROUND

INNER MIDDLE GROUND

WHITE RED

OUTER MIDDLE GROUND

WHITE RED

OUTER MIDDLE GROUND

OUTER MIDDLE GROUND

LEAVE TO PORT

LEAVE TO STARBOARD

BLACK
WHITE
RED

ISOLATED DANGER

BLACK & WHITE VERTICAL

LANDFALL BUOY

Buoys and marks of the international lateral system

top-marks; conical or diamond-shaped marks on starboard-hand buoys, and can or T-shaped marks on port-hand buoys.

In main channels, the buoys may be fitted with flashing lights, in which case starboard-hand buoys show a white light with an odd number of flashes and port-hand buoys even numbers in red or white. Spherical middle-ground buoys with red and white horizontal bands indicate that the main channel is to the right of the buoy, or that both sides of the buoy offer the same degree of safety. Spherical buoys painted with black

WRECK BUOY
(GREEN, WHITE LETTERS)

DAN BUOY

and white horizontal bands indicate that the main channel is to the left of the buoy.

Buoys that mark the middle of a channel may be of any shape, but not similar to port, starboard, or middle-ground buoys, and they are painted with black and white, or red and white vertical stripes. One of these buoys may be positioned way out at sea, as a landfall mark, to establish the position of the mariner when the shoreline is of a uniform character without conspicuous landmarks.

A spherical buoy similar to the mid-channel buoy is used to mark an isolated danger, such as a rock, but is then painted with wide black and red bands separated by a narrow horizontal white band.

Wrecks are marked by similar conical, can or spherical buoys, but painted green and with the word 'WRECK' in white letters. As with navigational buoys, their shape indicates the safe passage around them. If they are lighted, the colour of the light is green.

Metal radar reflectors are often fitted to navigational buoys so that radar-equipped vessels can obtain a stronger echo on their screen. Incidentally, it is an offence to land on, or to moor up to any navigational buoy.

MOORING BUOYS

Apart from navigational buoys, there are the numerous buoys used for the purpose of mooring ships, boats and seaplanes. They come in all sizes, shapes and colours, and can be identified by the ring on top, to which mooring warps, wires and chains can be attached.

MOORING PICK-UP BUOY

MOORING BUOY

Big-ship mooring buoys consist of a large steel cylinder supporting a heavy chain. The bottom end of the chain is secured to a massive weight on the sea bed, possibly heavy concrete blocks or old anchors. The steel cylinder may float in a vertical or horizontal attitude, with the mooring-ring on top. They may have timber battens or a circular timber fender around them, and they are usually black. Often they are numbered. They are large enough for a seaman to clamber aboard, which facilitates 'mooring up'. Smaller buoys of this type, intended for smaller coastal vessels, may not be stable enough to land on.

Buoys marking small boat and yacht moorings may be made of metal, but modern ones are more likely to be of plastics or cork. They do not always support a chain, but only the buoy rope; the chain, attached to the mooring weight or anchor, being allowed to lie on the bottom ready for hauling up by means of the buoy rope. The boat comes up to the mooring, and both buoy and buoy rope are hauled aboard by means of a boat-hook. The slack buoy rope is taken in quickly until one end of the chain arrives on deck and can be secured by turns around a samson post. Never pick up a mooring buoy and hang off the buoy rope. It not only chafes the rope, but if the rope breaks the mooring is lost.

Dan buoys or spar buoys are a distinctive type of buoy that may be seen lying around fishing harbours or, more likely, lashed to the rigging of a fishing-boat. From the illustration it will be obvious that it has been designed to be seen from a considerable distance. It consists basically of a long spar, weighted at the bottom end, with its buoyancy in the middle, and carrying a flag of some description at the top.

They are used by deep-sea fishermen to mark the ends of nets, etc, and by salvage vessels working offshore. In a rough sea, well away from the land, they can be seen against the sky when a normal buoy would be lost to sight in breaking water.

Fishing-net buoys come in several forms. The dark green glass spheres sometimes found cast up on the beach are buoys used in the fishing industry to support the headropes of fishing nets. In use, they have a coarse netting woven around them so that the buoy can be conveniently secured. Small metal and plastic buoys are also used for the same purpose.

Cork floats of many shapes are used by fishermen to support their nets and to mark the end of lobster-pot lines. Rough floats are made up of slabs of cork threaded on to tarred line, or round discs of cork normally used to support the headrope of fishing nets. In fact, any buoyant material supporting a light line, especially inshore in the vicinity of rocks, is most likely to be marking lobster or crab pots and must not be used to moor even the smallest of boats. Pots may each have their individual line and buoy, in which case there will probably be several dotted around in the same area, or a single buoy may be used to mark a long 'trot' of pots.

Small buoys of glass (*left*) or metal
are used to support
fishing nets

TROTS

The word 'trot' describes a number of things on a single line.
For instance, the fisherman's pots, or a series of moorings. In
the case of moorings, there would be a long, heavy chain on
the bottom, with several lighter rising chains secured to it at
suitable intervals by means of a swivel, each topped by a mooring buoy. The swivel allows a moored boat to swing on the tide,
without twisting the 'riser' into knots.

BEACONS AND LEADING MARKS

To guide boats and yachts through sandbanks and mudflats at
the entrance to small harbours, beacons, usually with an identifying top mark, are erected by the local authority, together
with leading marks ashore. Larger harbours also use this system, the beacons and leading marks carrying fixed, flashing,
white or coloured lights, for use at night.

    The beacon, or small lighthouse, may have a light which
shows different colours to seaward according to the direction

Cork floats are used
to mark the end of
lobster-pot lines

DETAIL OF A MOORING TROT

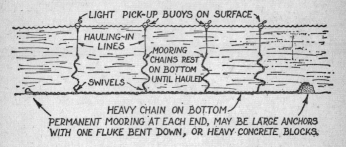

from which one is approaching. White is the usual colour which shows through the arc of safe approach, clear of all obstructions, and any change of colour to red or green warns the seaman that he is off the safe line of approach and must alter course back to the white sector.

Leading marks, which may be two beacons, one behind the other, or a white-painted rock to be kept in line with another conspicuous object, are called transits. When kept in line, they ensure clear passage past all obstructions.

In creeks and minor rivers used mainly by local boats, where the traffic does not warrant erection of permanent navigational aids, the deep-water channel may be marked by a succession of sticks or poles, known as 'withies' or 'perches', which follow

Leading marks are often two beacons, one behind the other

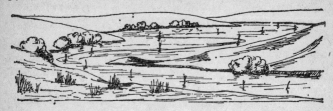

'Withies' or 'perches' mark the deep-water channel

the edge of the mud or sandbank. They should not be inter-
fered with, as someone has gone to considerable trouble to prevent small boats finishing up on the mud.

CHAPTER FOUR

Docks and Harbours

Docks and harbours provide a wealth of objects and structures to fascinate those with an interest in the sea, not to mention smells and odours that smack of ships, cargoes and faraway places.

GRAVING DOCKS

Not every harbour has a graving dock, but many larger ports will have at least one. It is, basically, a lock into which, when filled with water, a vessel can be floated, the lock gates closed and the water run off so that the ship is left standing in a dry dock. Bottom and side shoring timbers have to be carefully positioned so that the weight of the vessel is evenly supported, for while a ship is strong enough in its own element, its own weight can destroy it out of the water. Graving docks are so-called because they are mainly used for the purpose of 'graving', ie, cleaning off a ship's bottom.

A floating dock

NON-TIDAL BASINS AND DOCKS

These docks perform the opposite function to a graving dock – they enable a vessel to remain afloat in a harbour that dries out at low water. Many small coasters can safely be allowed to take the ground at low water – indeed, they are often designed with this in view – but large ocean-going ships would find themselves in all sorts of trouble and might well break their backs.

Ships can only enter or leave non-tidal docks during a limited period round about high water, the lock gates having to be closed as the tide begins to fall. Examples of non-tidal docks are those at Dover and Penzance for smaller craft, and the Port of London for large ships.

PORT OF LONDON

In prehistoric days, the River Thames was much broader and flanked by marshes which prevented access to the river except at one or two places. Near the site of the present London Bridge, a seam of gravel crossed the river and provided the first fordable point from the sea. It is a direct result of this ford that the City of London now stands where it is.

By the end of the second century, London was already a wealthy city, and during the reign of Canute it attained commercial supremacy in Britain. It was also the headquarters of the Navy, and the country's chief centre of ship-building.

In Elizabethan times, London handled fifty per cent of the country's trade, Southampton nine per cent, Newcastle five per cent, and Bristol three per cent. Liverpool and Cardiff had not by then come into any sort of prominence as ports.

The first wet dock with lock gates was built on the Thames by the East India Company during the middle of the seventeenth century for fitting out vessels launched from adjacent ship-building yards.

The steamship made its first appearance on the Thames in

1815, but it was not until 1875 that steam took first place from sail in the tonnage of vessels using the port.

In 1908, all the undertakings and powers of the various dock companies were taken over by the Port of London Authority, and, today, the port comprises sixty-nine miles of the tidal reaches of the Thames, from the No 1 Sea Reach buoy off Warden Point, in Kent, to the first full-tide lock at Teddington, in Middlesex.

Though London is not primarily a passenger port, as is Southampton, there are, nevertheless, two passenger terminals at Tilbury. The passenger landing-stage in the river is a floating structure, over a thousand feet long, and the largest passenger-carrying vessels can lie alongside it at any state of the tide.

The London and St Katherine docks are just outside the City of London, close by Tower Bridge. On the other side of the river, towards the sea, are the Surrey Commercial docks and, on the inside of the loop the river makes towards Greenwich, the West India and Millwall docks.

Farther down the river, on the northern bank, are the smaller East India docks and, ten miles seaward from London Bridge and forty miles from the sea, the Royal Victoria, Royal Albert, and King George V docks, known collectively as the Royal group. These Royal docks provide eleven miles of quays and the largest sheet of impounded dock water to be found anywhere in the world.

FLOATING DOCKS

A floating dock is a simple form of steel vessel, having double bottom and sides, into which water can be flooded or pumped out at will. The dock has a U-shaped section and is open at both ends. The double hull is partitioned off into many watertight compartments, and valves and pumps control the trim of the dock. By allowing water to flood into the chambers formed by the double sides and bottom, the dock sinks low enough in the water to allow a ship to be floated in. The water is then pumped out and the dock raises the vessel so that she is high and dry.

PATENT SLIPS

These provide another method of removing a vessel from its
element for the purposes of maintenance. A patent slip is in
the form of a large steel cradle which runs up and down an inclined permanent slipway on wheels and rails. At the lower

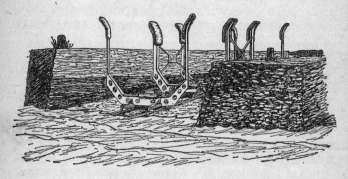

A patent slip with steel cradle on an inclined slipway

end of the slipway the cradle is submerged, allowing a boat to
be floated into the cradle and secured. A powerful windlass
then hauls the cradle, complete with boat, up the incline clear
of the water. Patent slips can usually take the coasting type of
vessel of up to 500 tons, and a few of the larger ones can handle
boats of up to 1,000 tons.

LAUNCHING SLIPWAYS

As their name implies, these are needed to transport some
thousands of tons of newly-built ship from the building-berth
safely into the water, only yards away. A lot of 'know how' is
called for in the process, and the launching of any ship is an
interesting experience that should not be missed. It provides an
exciting culmination to the months of slow building progress

from the laying of the keel onwards. From the building stocks, the 'ways' provide a 'one-way' ride down to the sea, prefaced in the case of a new ship by the launching ceremony, a bottle of champagne cracked across the bows and the traditional prayer, 'May God protect her and all who sail in her'.

Most large vessels are launched stern first, and their motion on becoming waterborne has to be arrested with drag wires and weights. A sideways launching technique, developed within the last few years, was originally confined to smaller vessels, such as fishing-boats and tugs, but is now being used for large ships.

GRIDS

Most harbours with a reasonably high rise and fall of the tide, have a grid structure on the bottom adjacent to the quay wall, or stout piles. Small vessels are floated alongside the quay wall, or piles, at high water, and the falling tide then leaves them high and dry, supported at intervals by the transverse baulks of timber, concrete slabs or steel rails that form the grid. The bottom of the ship's hull is then accessible between the supports and, by moving the boat a little on successive high tides, the entire hull can be dealt with.

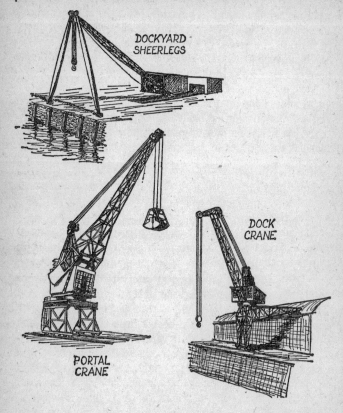

DOCKYARD
SHEERLEGS

DOCK
CRANE

PORTAL
CRANE

CRANES

The largest cranes can be seen around the ship-building yards,
handling machinery, pre-fabricated sections of hulls, superstructure, and all the heavy gear that goes into the building
and repairing of ships.

A crane is a self-contained lifting device, with its own
power and a winding drum for its lifting wire. They vary from
small, hand-operated ones, to the giant Magnus floating cranes
that will lift 800 tons. The most spectacular is the towering
'hammer-head' crane, with its great cantilever truss revolving

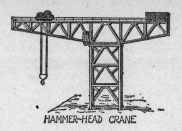

HAMMER-HEAD CRANE

against the sky. Then there is the portal jib crane that moves along on rails with traffic running through its lower structure, and the travelling gantry crane which may lift as much as 200 tons at a time.

The 'jib' is the boom of a crane pivoted from the bottom, and a derricking jib is a crane that can alter the angle of its jib by varying the length of the 'tie' between the crane post and the jib end, thereby altering its radius of action.

SHEER LEGS

Though also used for lifting heavy loads, sheer legs are a more simple structure than the familiar crane. They may only be of a temporary nature, rigged with stout spars and lashings, for a particular job, or they may be a permanent rig constructed of steel tubes forming a tripod of large dimensions, and capable of lifting a small vessel. The actual lift or load is taken by single or multi-part purchase blocks through which is rove rope or wire, which is then led to a convenient windlass.

DAVITS

Pronounced 'davids' by seamen, these are the small crane-like devices from which hang a ship's lifeboats. They are also used ashore on quay walls, for the convenient launching of small boats. Each davit has a block and tackle, usually in the form of a two-fold purchase, to provide the mechanical advantage required in lifting or lowering a fully-laden boat. Larger boats may require two treble blocks, forming a three-fold purchase to the 'boat falls', as the pulling end of the rope is called. Tackle, incidentally, is another seafaring word that is not pronounced as it is written. Seamen say 'taykle'.

Using the old-fashioned curved iron or steel davits, a boat may be swung inboard for snug stowage at sea, or swung outboard for lowering down into the water clear of the ship's side. This traditional type of davit has now been replaced on modern ships by mechanical davits that swing straight out in the vertical plane ready for lowering away.

The problem of launching ships' lifeboats from a founder-

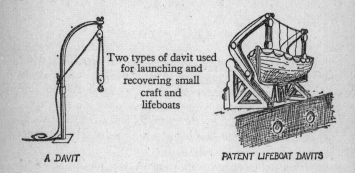

Two types of davit used for launching and recovering small craft and lifeboats

A DAVIT

PATENT LIFEBOAT DAVITS

ing vessel has always been fraught with danger and uncertainty. Invariably, a ship takes a heel or list to port or starboard as she fills up, or runs on a reef, so that only the life-boats on the low side can be launched.

The solution lies in having sufficient inflatable life-rafts for everyone on board, as these can then be thrown overboard and inflated by automatic CO_2 gas cylinders. If they land on anyone in the water, they are unlikely to cause injury, and people jumping into the life-rafts do not hurt themselves. They also provide more protection from the elements as they have rubberized canopies and can be equipped with the usual waterproofed rations, distress signals and radio transmitters.

ROUGH WEATHER BOOMS

Few harbours can shelter shipping from all winds, and sometimes a rough weather boom is floated across the entrance when weather conditions cause excessive motion inside the harbour. The heavy boom reduces the vertical component of the wave structure and breaks down the horizontal motion of any breaking seas. The general smoothing effect can be remarkable. Other small harbours slide steel shutters, or baulks of timber, down steel or masonry channels built into the harbour wall, closing off the entrance completely. When such harbours are closed to shipping, special signals are shown at the pier head.

FENDERS

To prevent damage to the hull of any vessel lying alongside a quay wall, pier, or wooden piles, resilient fendering is required. This fendering varies from lengths of old rope, old motor-car tyres, baulks of timber, etc, to elaborate and expensive pneumatic rubber fendering, which looks like lorry wheels clamped together and is free to revolve with the movement of the ship.

Yachts and other small vessels that may have to lie alongside each other also have a fendering problem. They are well catered for with smart, canvas-covered sponge, or pneumatic plastic 'fend-offs' of various designs. Tradition amongst

RUBBER DOCK FENDERING

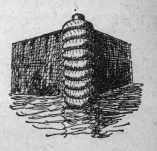

Right: revolving rubber fendering on a dock corner

yachtsmen decrees that all fend-offs are inboard when under way, though the working boat will often be seen with old tyre or rope fend-offs hanging over the side – and no shame at all.

TIDE GAUGES

In many harbours, especially those that dry out to some extent, one can often see a tide gauge mounted vertically against the quay or the pier end, painted black or white, and marked off in feet from the harbour bottom. The depth of water available can then be seen at a glance.

All waters connected to the open sea and below high-water level are subject to the rise and fall of the tides. This vertical movement of the oceans is the result of the sum of the gravitational pull of the sun and the moon, and the moon being so much nearer, despite its smaller mass, has by far the greater effect.

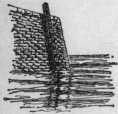

A tide gauge

When the moon is full, or new, the sun and moon are both pulling together and produce the highest of the high tides and the lowest of the low tides. During the half-moon period, the tides do not rise so high or fall so low and this period, which lasts roughly a week, is known as 'neap' tides. The period of high tides also lasts a week and is called 'spring' tides.

Configuration of the land mass and the position of islands, can produce unusual tidal effects. Due mainly to the position of the Isle of Wight, Southampton and the Solent area have a double high water every twelve hours, whereas in most parts the tide rises to the highest level and then begins to fall steadily to low water approximately six hours later.

The tide does not rise and fall at a uniform rate, but starts slowly from high or low water, speeding up to maximum at half-tide and then slowing down again to zero at the turn of the tide. During the first hour of the tide it rises or falls one-twelfth of the tidal range for the particular tide, two-twelfths during the second hour, three-twelfths during both the third

DIRECTION OF THE MAIN STREAM OF FLOOD TIDE ROUND THE BRITISH ISLES

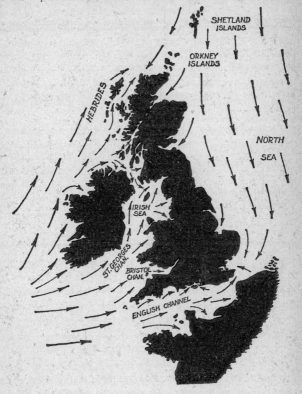

and fourth hours, slowing down to two-twelfths during the fifth hour, and one-twelfth again for the last hour.

HARBOUR MASTER

The harbour master is in charge of the day-to-day management of the harbour, usually under the direction of harbour commissioners. His office will be found conveniently near the harbour, and anyone wishing to make use of the harbour facilities is required to do so through the harbour office. As the harbour master has a responsibility equivalent to the command of a ship, it is customary in large ports to give him the courtesy title of 'Captain'. This courtesy title does not automatically go with a master mariner's certificate – though many harbour masters are so qualified – but with a command. In borderline cases, however, such as large yachts and small working vessels, possession of a master's certificate would tend to make the subtle distinction between the familiar 'Skipper' or the more formal 'Captain'.

There is often misunderstanding regarding the rank of captain in the Royal Navy and the Army. Both Naval and military captains may not necessarily ever have held commands – they might be medical officers, engineers or administrative officers – but a Lieutenant RN may hold a responsible sea-going command.

MARINE BAROMETER

The weather plays an all-important part in the lives of seafarers and in, or near, the harbour master's office may usually be seen a marine barometer. It will be a mercurial barometer, which is more accurate than the more popular aneroid barometer used ashore. Its greater accuracy is only of value to the meteorologist in plotting his synoptic weather chart, but it is useful to recognize it for what it is and to be able to read it. If it is outside, it will be in a glass-fronted case.

The barometer itself consists of a glass tube filled with mercury, mounted in a brass tube and suspended in gimbals. The top of the glass tube is exposed through a slit in the metal case, so that the height of the mercury can be observed. The metal case has a scale calibrated in fractions of an inch, with a vernier attachment giving an accuracy down to one-thousandth of an inch. Also attached to the metal

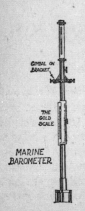

GIMBAL ON
BRACKET

THE
GOLD
SCALE

MARINE
BAROMETER

case is a thermometer, which may include a 'gold slide scale' combined with another sliding scale for correction of height above sea level and latitude.

HYGROMETER

Weather prediction calls for a knowledge of the relative humidity of the air, as well as its pressure, and there may well be a 'Stevenson screen' in the vicinity of the barometer. This is simply a wooden cabinet with louvred sides and front, which protects the hygrometer inside from direct sunlight or rain but allows free access to the atmosphere.

The hygrometer itself, known as 'Mason's hygrometer', consists of two thermometers alongside each other. The bulb of one thermometer is wrapped in cambric material and has a wick leading down into a small cup of water. When the weather is dry there is a degree of evaporation round the bulb of the wet thermometer, and due to the latent heat of evaporation, there is a drop in temperature. The difference in temperature readings between the dry thermometer and the wet thermometer bears a direct relation to the relative humidity of the atmosphere.

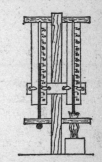

THE HYGROMETER

CUSTOMS HOUSE

The more important harbours will have a Customs House, and some of these are of great historic interest. In the Devonshire port of Dartmouth, for example, the Customs House was built in 1739 on the quay in Bayards Cove from which the Pilgrim Fathers set sail in the *Mayflower* in their search for a new world.

The duties of a Customs officer include visiting all ships arriving from foreign ports, levying duties on certain imports,

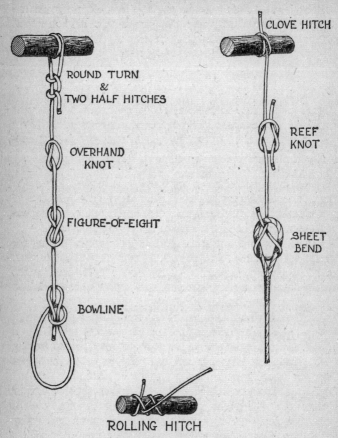

ROUND TURN
&
TWO HALF HITCHES

OVERHAND
KNOT

FIGURE-OF-EIGHT

BOWLINE

CLOVE HITCH

REEF
KNOT

SHEET
BEND

ROLLING HITCH

Knots and hitches commonly used to secure ropes or to join
two together

and taking preventive measures against smuggling. The Registrar of Shipping is also to be found at the Customs House,
together with the Receiver of Wreck.

All British ships and yachts of over fifteen tons gross are
required to be registered as British ships by the Registrar of
Shipping. This entails internal measurements of the hull, and

after allowable deductions for engine space, etc, the registered tonnage is arrived at. This is then carved on a main structural beam and is the tonnage which determines the amount a ship is charged for harbour dues, light dues, etc.

RECEIVER OF WRECK

It comes as a surprise to many people to learn that all wrecks belong to someone, and that to interfere with a wreck or remove parts of it, without permission of the owner and notification to the Receiver of Wreck, is a punishable offence.

Any ship that has sunk in such a position that it becomes a danger to navigation must be buoyed and marked, unless the owner decides legally to abandon the wreck, in which case the port authorities concerned must be notified. An owner cannot abandon a vessel that has sunk as a result of negligence.

It is an offence to salve a portion of a wreck, leaving the remainder in any port, harbour, channel or navigable river. And as the entire coastline of the British Isles comes under some authority or other, the owner of a wreck may well find himself saddled with a 'white elephant'.

The authority concerned can remove a wreck that has not been officially abandoned and recover the cost of doing so from the owner, or the person who was negligent in sinking her. This same authority also has first charge on the wreck for any costs involved.

When a wreck is found at sea it becomes 'droits of Admiralty' and these include things left floating from a perished ship (flotsam); things thrown overboard to save a ship that has perished (jetsam); things thrown overboard with a buoy attached, from a ship that has perished (ligan); and a ship which has been abandoned without hope of return (derelict). There are no 'droits' unless the ship has perished. And only on being landed or floating ashore do they become wreck.

All 'droits' and wreck must be handed over to the Receiver of Wreck under penalty of £100, forfeiture of salvage claim, and payment of double the value to the original owner. It is also an offence (maximum sentence: five years' penal servitude) to take 'droits' or wreck found within three miles of the coast to a foreign port for sale.

An owner of 'droits' or wreck can claim them back from the Receiver of Wreck within one year of their coming into the Receiver's possession, but he is responsible for any salvage claims. Any person finding his own property as wreck is not bound to hand it over to the Receiver, but must supply him with a full description and any marks of identity.

DIVING

Any underwater work being carried out by divers in docks and harbours presents an excellent opportunity of seeing them in action, especially if they are working off the quay wall. The modern diver must be a 'jack of all trades' for he is called upon to do a variety of jobs. It might be salvage work, or clearance of wreck, construction or maintenance of harbour installations – such as work on moorings or lock gates – or surveys and repairs to ships' hulls.

The diver is not paid to go down and look around, or feel around – the water is usually black in harbours – but to get on with the job. A good diver will have learned to live underwater, and he can use all the normal hand tools. Hammers, pickaxes, drills, knives and so on can all be used underwater as easily as on the surface, and even pneumatic-powered tools can be taken below.

Basically, there are three types of diving apparatus. There is the standard gear, which utilizes the traditional metal helmet secured to a watertight, rubberized twill dress, together with twenty-pound lead boots, two forty-pound leads on chest and back, and fed with air by hose from the surface. The second type is the aqualung compressed-air apparatus, which can be used with or without independent rubber suit. The third type is the oxygen re-breathing apparatus, which is similar to that worn by wartime frogmen. The latter has the operational advantage of not giving off a continual stream of bubbles.

Standard diving gear is by far the most comfortable, when long periods have to be spent underwater, and has the advan-

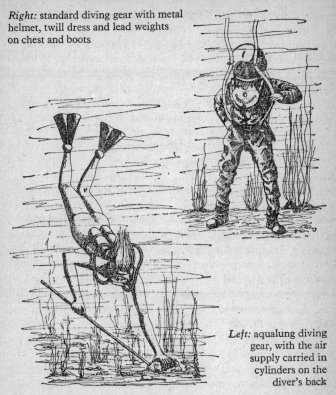

Right: standard diving gear with metal helmet, twill dress and lead weights on chest and boots

Left: aqualung diving gear, with the air supply carried in cylinders on the diver's back

tage of reliable, two-way, telephonic communication. Unfortunately, it is heavy and cumbersome out of the water, the total weight of all the gear being about 180 pounds.

Aqualung compressed-air apparatus, being much lighter and self-contained, is used mainly by sporting divers, though professional divers may employ it occasionally for the less gruelling work. The air supply, compressed to a pressure between 2,000 and 3,000 psi, is carried in cylinders which are worn on the diver's back.

Oxygen re-breathing apparatus is for the expert only, and cannot be used by a diver employed under Factory Act conditions except with permission of the factory inspector. Self-employed divers can, of course, use it, but it has a depth limitation of thirty-three feet, except for descents of very short duration. However, it does come into its own for shallow-water diving, when supplies of clean, compressed air at 2,000 psi are not available for the filling of aqualungs.

There are also variations of the three basic types of diving gear. The standard diving apparatus, specially designed for work at great depths and using oxygen helium mixtures, employs soda lime to remove the carbon dioxide produced by the diver, as does the shallow-water, oxygen re-breathing apparatus. Oxygen and helium are used instead of air, as the nitrogen in air produces a form of narcosis at depths below 150 feet. The soda lime is necessary, as even the smallest amount of carbon dioxide will tend to promote asphyxiation at great depths, and aggravates the onset of the 'bends', the diver's occupational hazard.

The more simple aqualung apparatus can be modified by feeding the demand valve with low-pressure air from the surface by means of a light hosepipe, so dispensing with the need for high-pressure cylinders. This is a handy rig for the working diver and, like the standard gear, has the advantage of unlimited duration.

When trained in the use of all three types of apparatus and fully qualified, a diver may then be issued with a British master diver's certificate – the hallmark of a professional, working diver.

DIVING AS A SPORT

Diving is a sport that cannot be taken lightly, and is comparable with such pastimes as flying, climbing and motor racing, all of which have their hazards. In land sports, however, the dangers are obvious, whereas underwater swimmers have to be wary of the more insidious risks inherent in diving physiology. Fortunately for the diver, to know these risks is to understand them and to realize that they can all be avoided by the use of common-sense and a little care. Underwater swimming should not be practised as a violent activity, but in a quiet, graceful manner. Often the indifferent swimmer will get more pleasure and satisfaction from submarine exploration than the powerful competition performer who frequently insists on steaming around, missing everything of interest and using up air fast.

Self-tuition in snorkel diving is quite practicable, and it is not impossible to become a good aqualung diver without professional instruction, but, since a cautious approach to this great sport is most desirable, an initial course of training at a diving school is much to be recommended.

There are a number of underwater clubs and groups in Great Britain, fourteen of them in association with the British Underwater Centre at Dartmouth, Devon, forming the Association of British Underwater Clubs. All these clubs believe in the principle of individual self-reliance, which has been developed to achieve maximum safety in our thicker, tidal waters. They undertake that their members will always wear a CO_2 lifejacket, and make use of a safety boat when diving in open waters.

There are other clubs outside the Association, some of which practice the British method, and some, like the British Sub-Aqua Club, which sponsor the 'buddy diving' technique, an import from the Mediterranean, and practised, in theory at least, in the clearer 'playboy' waters of the world.

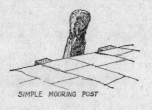

SIMPLE MOORING POST

CHAPTER FIVE

Ships of All Sizes

The largest vessels, until recent times, were the ocean-going liners – the passenger-carrying vessels of the world – maintaining a regular service between particular ports. But during the last few years giant tankers have been built, like the *Nissio Maru* of 132,334 tons, the *Tokyo Maru*, 150,000 tons, and the *Idemitsu Maru*, which carries 210,000 tons of oil on every voyage from the Persian Gulf to Japan yet requires a crew of only thirty-two officers and men. Tankers are measured in deadweight, which indicates the amount of cargo or fuel carried by the ship and this often leads to confusion when comparing the size of a tanker with that of a passenger ship whose gross tonnage is measured by different standards, with one

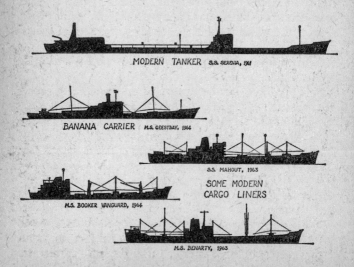

MODERN TANKER   S.S. SERENIA, 1961

BANANA CARRIER   M.S. GEESTBAY, 1964

S.S. MAHOUT, 1963

SOME MODERN
CARGO LINERS

M.S. BOOKER VANGUARD, 1964

M.S. BENARTY, 1963

gross ton equalling 100 cubic feet of permanently enclosed space. Even so, a 200,000-ton tanker is much bigger than the 82,998-ton *Queen Elizabeth*, the world's largest passenger liner.

Shell International have had three 165,000-ton tankers built by the Japanese, who also built a similar one for Germany. These ships, although only twenty feet longer than the *Queen Mary* and the *Queen Elizabeth*, have thirty-seven feet more beam and draw fourteen feet more water.

But even these huge ships are soon to be eclipsed. By late 1968, 312,000-ton tankers, more than twice the size of the ill-fated *Torrey Canyon*, will be calling regularly at a new oil storage depot in Bantry Bay, in South-West Ireland. Lloyd's Register is making studies for a 500,000-ton tanker, and one British shipyard has announced that it will even build a million-ton tanker if anyone wants it.

Cunard's new passenger liner, the *Queen Elizabeth II*, built by John Brown & Co, is a twin-screw, single funnel, steamship of 58,000 tons, with a length of 960 feet, beam 104 feet, and a draft of 31 feet.

Smaller editions of the ocean liners are the cross-Channel passenger boats, which also carry a limited amount of cargo, while among the most attractive-looking ships must be counted the large cruise steamers, with their spacious promenade decks, and the white-painted, fruit-carrying ships that work out to the Mediterranean and the Caribbean Sea.

Freight-carriers can be spotted by the presence of cargo-handling derricks on the masts, and large hatchways for loading and discharging cargo. Derricks vary in their lifting capacity, but the average is about ten tons for general cargo, though there is usually a 'jumbo' derrick on the mainmast that can cope with around fifty tons. However, the size and type of derricks and cranes vary from ship to ship, the 'Stulken' derrick installed on the M V *Sharistan* being able to lift no less than 180 tons.

The term 'tramp-steamer' is often mistakenly believed to refer to a certain type of vessel, whereas, in fact, the word 'tramp' describes what many of these freight-carriers are

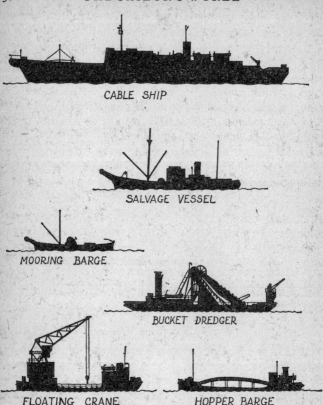

CABLE SHIP

SALVAGE VESSEL

MOORING BARGE

BUCKET DREDGER

FLOATING CRANE

HOPPER BARGE

doing – 'tramping' about the world, picking up general cargo wherever they can and delivering it to ports, large and small, anywhere. The picture conjured up of a disreputable, dirty old ship, flying a faded red ensign, can be a distortion indeed, as some very smart and efficient ships are in the tramping business.

Tankers are easily recognizable, as they describe themselves. Great long ships with tank tops and valves in lieu of cargo hatches and derricks; engines and accommodation right aft, they vary in size from quite small local boats to giants of over 200,000 tons deadweight.

Ships are designed to suit the special purposes for which they are built. Amongst the largest, apart from tankers and aircraft-carriers, are the bulk carriers for grain, etc, refrigerated ships bringing frozen meat from the other side of the world, and, coming down in size, the roll-on-roll-off car and train ferries, fishing trawlers and drifters, colliers, pilot vessels – all of them playing their special part in the maritime scene.

PADDLE–STEAMERS

With their great beam and shallow draft, these old-timers have served us well, but their days are nearly done and only a few examples are still working in our waters. For many years they operated from piers in exposed, comparatively shallow bays, carrying up to 2,000 passengers at a time on holiday excursions. With their paddle-wheels mounted amidships they have excellent manoeuvring ability, and no propellers to be fouled by lines or wires.

Paddle-wheel steamers were still being built just before the Second World War, a 200-foot excursion steamer having been built in 1937 and put into service in the Bournemouth area. Most of the paddle-steamers still afloat are about fifty years old, but some still push along at twenty knots, which is fast for vessels of this size.

CABLE SHIPS

These ships are built for the special purpose of laying submarine cables, having their bows and sterns designed to facilitate the hauling and veering of cable, and holds which can stow many miles of the cable itself. The bows of a cable ship are usually of the 'clipper' form, carrying rollers at the stemhead.

One of the latest types of cable ships is the *Retriever* of

8,000 tons. Her two funnels are abreast of each other, instead of being arranged fore and aft, as in most ships. This allows the cable to have a clear run through the superstructure, from bow to stern. This type of vessel was used to lay the 28,000 miles of Commonwealth Round-the-World telephone system.

SALVAGE VESSELS

Although we refer to the powerful, ocean-going tugs as salvage vessels, there are also the lifting salvage vessels of rather similar design to the larger cable ships but with special bows and lifting gear for raising wrecks and for handling big-ship moorings, anchors, etc.

Most of their work is around the coast and in harbours, and their size is measured in hundreds of tons rather than the thousands of tons of the cable ships. Admiralty salvage vessels come into this class of ship, but are slightly larger, being around 1,000 tons and usually looking smarter – but then they do not have to earn their own living.

WEATHER SHIPS

The British weather ships operate out of Great Harbour, Greenock, on the west coast of Scotland, and spend just over a month at sea, twenty-four days actually on station.

Originally, in 1954, the British weather ships stationed out in the North Atlantic were ex-Naval corvettes, but by 1961 they had been replaced by ex-Naval frigates. They are commanded by Merchant Navy officers and carry a total crew of fifty-six, including radio/radar operators and meteorologists.

Four weather stations are maintained by Britain, Netherlands and France, and one of the four stations is maintained with the additional services of a Norwegian weather ship.

On station, the weather ships can be likened to a floating island in the North Atlantic. Meteorological observations are made every three hours and radioed to shore stations. They also provide search and rescue services and navigational aids for aircraft.

SMALL CRAFT SILHOUETTES

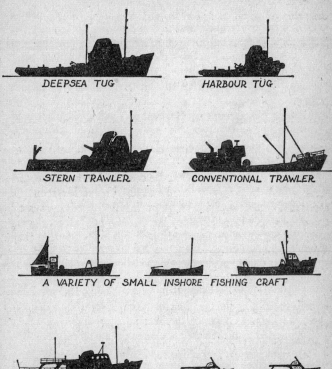

DEEPSEA TUG

HARBOUR TUG

STERN TRAWLER

CONVENTIONAL TRAWLER

A VARIETY OF SMALL INSHORE FISHING CRAFT

LARGE MOTOR YACHT

FAST CABIN CRUISERS

CABIN CRUISERS

MOTOR SAILER

Tugs, trawlers, inshore fishing craft and some typical yachts
and cabin cruisers

OIL RIGS

With the discovery of natural gas, and perhaps oil, under the North Sea, a new and interesting structure can now be seen off the east coast of Britain – the offshore oil rig. The latest type of rig can drill down through the sea bed whilst it is still afloat, or it can sink itself so that it stands firmly on the sea bottom.

The *Sea Quest*, built by Harland & Wolff of Belfast, is of this semi-submersible type and represents the latest development in the recovery of gas and oil from under the sea. In her normal floating position for towing, the rig draws twenty-three feet of water. By flooding her legs with up to 12,700 tons of water, she can be adjusted to a floating drilling position with her pontoons eighty feet below the surface, or she can stand on her own legs in up to 110 feet of water.

When operating in a floating position, nine anchors, each weighing 30,000 pounds, are required to hold her steady. On the main deck, a two-level, steel deckhouse is mounted, surmounted by a helicopter landing-deck. Also on the main deck are deckhouses enclosing the drilling machinery, and a drilling mast 155 feet high. The control room is located under the main working deck aft of the accommodation house, and a well-equipped workshop situated in the engine room.

A special system of helicopter landing lighting is provided to meet Board of Trade requirements. Navigation lights, comprising one flashing red, and two flashing white lights, are carried on the three caissons, together with a fog signal with a range of two miles.

TUGS

Tugs are vessels which have been specially designed to suit the duties for which they are intended. Powerfully-engined, they are recognizable by their clear decks aft, low 'freeboard' and towing rails running athwartships. Large ocean-going tugs, fitted with powerful automatic towing winches and hooks, tow

Tugs have to push as well
as pull — hence the rope
fender on the bows

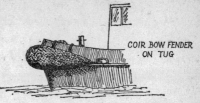

COIR BOW FENDER
ON TUG

our largest vessels, dry docks, etc, from one side of the world to the other.

On the after deck, one on each quarter, are mounted strong posts known as 'malogger posts', which support large folding vertical and horizontal rollers that act as 'fairleads' to the towing wire when manoeuvring, and stow down on deck when not in use.

Distinguished by their short-ended 'chunky' appearance are the smaller harbour and dock tugs used in the berthing of large vessels, and for local towing of dumb barges and lighters. These tugs have to push as well as pull, so they have large 'bow fenders', usually made of rope.

When towing from amidship hooks, there is always the danger of the relatively small tug getting herself broadside on to the much larger tow — known as 'girting', or becoming 'girt'. Any strain on the tow rope under these conditions is likely to result in the tug 'turning turtle'. To reduce this risk of becoming 'girt', a rope called a 'gob rope' is led from each quarter and over the tow rope, bowsing it down and keeping the pull aft.

Towage requires a special knowledge of seamanship, and there are special signals provided in the International Code of Signals for use only when towing. By day, the International Code flag 'A' or, at night, the letter 'A' ($\cdot$ —) flashed in morse code, means 'Is towing hawser fast?' when sent by the tug, or 'Towing hawser is fast' when sent by the towed vessel. The letter 'R' means 'I will go slower', when sent from the tug, or 'Go slower', when sent by the towed vessel. Special sound signals have also been adopted by the port of Liverpool for use between vessels towing or under tow. Signals to tugs ahead are made by mouth whistle, and to those astern, by ship's whistle, each signal being repeated back by the tug.

BARGES

These are flat-bottomed boats built for carrying freight, except in the Royal Navy, where a 'barge' is the term applied to a man-of-war's second boat for the use of senior officers.

Most people will think of the ugly 'swim-headed' dumb barges, barges without any means of propulsion that are towed around our harbours and rivers, or perhaps the more attractive 'narrow boat' of our inland waterways. But until recently there were the picturesque, if not beautiful, Thames sailing barges which used to work between London and our east coast ports. Just before the last war, the author can remember seeing thirty-two of them under full sail, under conditions of very little wind, drifting past Pin Mill on the River Orwell bound from Ipswich down to the sea. It was a picture never to be forgotten – and never seen again.

There were two types of Thames barge, one intended for river work and a slightly larger one for sea service. They were very nearly the last working sailing ships, and most of them were 'spritsail' rigged, which means that the main boom ran from the 'spider band' on the mainmast to the 'peak' of the mainsail. The Thames 'River' class boats had a smaller mizzen sail and no bowsprit. Some of the seagoing Thames barges had a boom for the mainsail in the more usual position – along the foot of the sail – and these were called 'boomies'.

Thames barges are mentioned because they can still be seen occasionally, sailing as yachts or moored up as houseboats, and there may be a few demasted ones working as motor barges.

Sailing barges have flat bottoms so that they can take the ground, but their main distinguishing feature are the 'lee boards' mounted amidships, one on either side of the vessel. These are flat boards that can be swung down to form a fore and aft keel surface on either side of the boat. When sailing, the board on the lee, or downwind side is lowered, the board

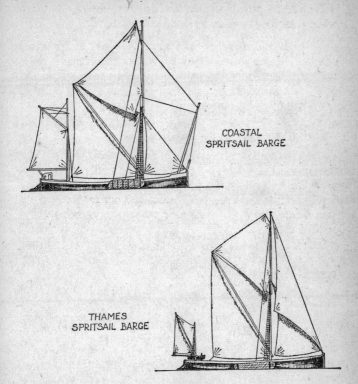

COASTAL
SPRITSAIL BARGE

THAMES
SPRITSAIL BARGE

on the windward side being hove up with tackle, clear of the water.

Quite a few barge yachts are to be seen in our waters, but most of these originate from Holland. They are the Dutch barges, noted for their curved lines, bluff bows and solid construction. There are several types as the Dutch build some for inland waters and others as seagoing vessels. The latter are built with stout timbers to withstand the pounding of beaching along the open coast of Holland. The 'Schokker' with its acutely-raked stem, curved gaff and loose-footed mainsail is one of these. Other well-known types of Dutch barge include the Boier, Botter, Hoogars, Hengst and Tjotter.

MOORING BARGES

Most harbours have their own mooring vessel, either in the form of a dumb barge or pontoon, with a characteristic roller fairlead. These mooring barges can only handle yacht and small-boat moorings, the larger salvage vessels being called in to overhaul big-ship moorings.

FISHING-BOATS

These really do come in all shapes and sizes, depending on the waters they navigate and the type of fishing carried out. They include trawlers, drifters, seine-netters, longliners, shrimpers, crabbers, and many others.

A type of deep-sea fishing vessel now coming into more general use is the stern trawler, which allows the trawl and the catch to be power-winched right inboard over the stern, saving the heavy work of manhandling the net and catch alongside and over the rail.

From quite a distance, the home port of a fishing vessel can be determined from the registration letters and numbers on the bows. The boat's individual number is preceded by one or two letters, the first letter being the first letter of the name of the port in which she is registered, and any second letter being the last letter of the port's name. Thus a fishing-boat from Brixham carries the letters 'BM', and one from Dartmouth 'DH', and so on. Only registered fishing-boats are allowed by law to sell their catch, but any boat may fish without being registered, if the catch is not for resale.

DREDGERS

Again, these are specially-built ships, and they can often be seen working, and certainly heard, in our harbours, estuaries and rivers, keeping the shipping channels deep enough for the type of vessels using the port.

The entrance to harbours at the mouth of a river tends to silt up quickly, especially when it is wide at the mouth, as the fast-flowing river water carries with it tons of mud and sand in suspension. As the current slackens on reaching the open sea the sand and mud are deposited in banks and, unless removed, will in time form a 'bar' across the entrance. Sand deposits will also tend to form banks where a prevailing tidal current slackens or alters direction, and in both cases the services of a dredger is the only answer.

The 'spoil' may be dredged up by means of an endless chain of buckets, a grab, a suction pipe, or even a dipper bucket similar to a land excavator. The dredged-up soil has then to be got rid of, which sometimes presents a problem. Some of the larger dredgers, which may run to 4,000 tons displacement, feed it into their own hull and, having their own propulsive power, can steam out to sea to a dumping ground, where the spoil is unloaded by opening the hoppers in the bottom of the vessel.

Smaller dredgers may consist only of a pontoon hull. These have to be moved around by tugs, and the spoil they dredge up is loaded into hopper barges alongside.

Bucket dredges can work down to a depth of sixty feet or more, each bucket holding between twenty and thirty cubic feet of spoil and lifting about 1,000 cubic feet an hour.

Suction dredgers have more the appearance of a normal ship, as the suction pipe, which is lowered to the sea bottom, is not so conspicuous or as noisy as the chain of buckets in the bucket dredger. Some suction dredgers include a revolving cutter at the nozzle end of the pipe for cutting into clay.

Yet another form of dredger is the reclamation dredger, which is designed to build up banks rather than to clear channels. It sucks up the spoil and then discharges it at a distance by pipeline or conveyor to the point where it is required. This type of dredger is usually of the pontoon variety and without means of self-propulsion.

HOVERCRAFT

The hovercraft is quite a newcomer to the maritime scene. It neither floats nor flies in the conventional ways, but it is supported on a cushion of air trapped between itself and the surface. It has the disadvantage of requiring high power/weight ratio engines, with high fuel consumptions, and expert maintenance of a standard similar to the modern aircraft. In the world of boats and shipping, it is a fragile structure. Its advantages are its speed over the water and its ability, in certain types, to travel with equal ease over land and water and many knowledgeable people consider it a remarkable invention of infinite promise.

Low-pressure blowers or fans produce a cushion of air beneath the craft so that it is borne up just clear of the surface over which it is travelling. A secondary source of power is required to move it horizontally, and this is normally provided by engine-driven aircraft-type propellers. To improve its efficiency, a flexible and somewhat vulnerable skirt is employed to contain the cushion of air on which it is supported.

The largest hovercraft yet built is the £1,750,000 British Hovercraft Development Corporation's SRN 4 which is of 165 tons, 130 feet in length and able to carry up to 800 people at 80 mph.

HYDROFOILS

The hydrofoil hull has now been developed to the stage of being a practicable high-speed, passenger-carrying vessel, but it is still confined mainly to inland waters and sheltered seas.

The hydrofoil boat has an immersed hull to support it at rest, but it also has streamlined legs which extend down into the water carrying small hydrofoils shaped like the wing of an aeroplane. When the vessel is propelled forwards at speed, these hydrofoils raise the main hull completely clear of the water so that the vessel is unaffected by rough surface conditions and provides a smoother and faster ride than any surface-borne vessel.

For certain purposes, such as the operation of fast ferry services in sheltered waters, the hydrofoil vessel has proved its worth and a number of these craft are in regular service in many parts of the world, including the Mediterranean, Scandinavia, Venezuela, Canada, the U S S R and Japan.

STEEL SHIPS

The strength of a steel ship is in its shape, which is in the form of a box section. The keel and bottom plates, the sides (called the shell plating) and the decks, form a stiff girder which resists bending. Move either one of them and the whole structure would collapse. Steel is used exclusively, except for small vessels, and much use is made of welding and riveting processes to bind the plates, frames, beams and angles together.

SHIP SHAPES

The simplest form of ship has 'flush' decks, which means that the main deck runs straight without a break from bow to stern, the superstructure, such as the 'bridge' and above-deck accommodation, being superimposed upon it.

A common type of vessel is the 'three island' design with raised bow, raised midship section and raised stern. Such a ship will have her engines and main accommodation amidships.

The smaller European cargo-carrier may be of the 'raised quarterdeck' type, with engines aft and the bridge at the break in the deck line.

Smaller working boats, common around our shores, are the 'poop-decked' coasters of around 500 tons. Their bridge, accommodation and engines are located right aft, leaving large holds and hatchways amidships. Many of this type are British-owned, but more of them hail from Continental and Scandinavian countries, especially Holland.

CHAPTER SIX

Ships of the Royal Navy

Painted in the standard Service grey, there can be no mistake about ships of the Royal Navy, and their shape and armament tell their own tale.

Gone are the days of the giant, armoured battleships, the *Vanguard* of 44,500 tons having been the last of the breed. Now the aircraft-carrier is capable of delivering a much bigger punch at a greater range than the largest Naval gun ever devised. The aircraft-carrier HMS *Eagle* is a ship of 36,000 tons, but there are also smaller carriers of 22,000 and 13,000 tons.

Next in size of Naval vessels are the cruisers, which range from 5,000 to 9,000 tons and are followed by the 2,600-ton minelayers and fleet escort ships.

'Battle' class destroyers are over 2,400 tons, and various classes of frigates range between 1,000 and 2,000 tons.

Submarines, as we see them afloat on the surface, do not look very large, but like icebergs, their real bulk is below the surface of the water – a thousand tons or more. Our largest submarines will be the nuclear-powered 'Resolution' class of over 7,500 tons and designed to carry sixteen Polaris missiles.

The *Dreadnought* which is a prototype nuclear-powered 'hunter' type of submarine, has a displacement, when afloat on the surface, of 3,500 tons. Her hull is shaped like the back of a whale, and she has a streamlined conning-tower looking like the dorsal fin of a fish. During turns, she banks over, having controls similar to those of an aircraft. The 'Valiant' class of nuclear-powered 'hunter' submarines will be even larger than the *Dreadnought*. The 'Porpoise' class is Britain's largest conventional type of submarine, with a tonnage of 1,500. Then

WARSHIP SILHOUETTES

AIRCRAFT CARRIER

"COUNTY" CLASS GUIDED MISSILE DESTROYER

GUNBOAT

"SALISBURY" CLASS AIRCRAFT DIRECTION FRIGATE

"LEOPARD" CLASS ANTI-AIRCRAFT FRIGATE

TYPE 15 ANTI-SUBMARINE FRIGATE

"WHITBY" CLASS ANTI-SUBMARINE FRIGATE

"A" CLASS SUBMARINE

SURVEY VESSEL

CRUISERS H.M.S. "BLAKE", "LION" & "TIGER"

COASTAL MINESWEEPER

BATTLESHIP H.M.S. "VANGUARD"

Representative types, drawn to scale, of twelve classes of ships
in the Royal Navy

comes the 'A' class of 1,120 tons, and the 'S' class of just under 1,000 tons. The smallest submarine is the 'Explorer' class, which, although small, is fast. It can travel at twenty-four knots underwater, using a special fuel. Finally, the smallest of our conventional submarines are the 'Midget' class, displacing only thirty tons and fifty-four feet in length.

Minesweepers come in three sizes: the ocean minesweeper of 1,000 tons, the coastal minesweeper of 360 tons, and the wooden-hulled inshore minesweeper of 100 tons.

Apart from the Royal Naval depot ships of 11,000 tons, the remaining classes comprise small vessels, such as the fast patrol boats 'Bold' and 'Gay' classes, the seaward defence 'Ford' class, and the old wartime 'B' class motor launches (MLs) and harbour duty launches (HDMLs), both of which, when surplus to Navy requirements, have been converted in large numbers into motor yachts and passenger-carrying vessels.

Used as tenders to the larger ships and for sea training are several small classes of Naval boats, such as admirals' barges, picket boats, whalers, gigs, launches, etc, mostly names peculiar to the senior service.

After the Second World War the days of the Royal Navy as the most important of the armed forces seemed to be numbered but, with the advent of nuclear submarines and their unprecedented striking power, they would now seem to be back in the 'front line' and likely to remain there.

ROYAL AIR FORCE MARINE SECTION

The most youthful service, the Royal Air Force, also goes to sea and has a sizeable fleet of its own, comprising vessels of various types designed for special duties.

The major RAF marine depot is at Mountbatten, Plymouth, where in the old days 'Sunderland' flying boats could be seen at their moorings. Seaplanes and flying boats are no longer in service with the RAF, but there are still the various bombing and gunnery ranges out at sea to supervise, and their high-speed air-sea rescue craft will always be needed.

There is also the Air Ministry Mooring and Salvage Section,

now much smaller than it once was. It is manned by civilian employees of the Air Ministry and carries out the maintenance work suggested by its title. Various vessels are employed, some of them about 500 tons, such as the *Rafmoor* working out of Weymouth in Dorset.

CHAPTER SEVEN

Yachts and Small Boats

YACHTS

The word 'yacht' came from the Dutch and, as used by us to-day, describes a vessel used for pleasure purposes. Quite small, decked, sailing boats, providing some accommodation for the crew, are referred to as 'yachts', but small power vessels under forty-five feet in length would more likely be referred to as 'motor cruisers' – the term 'motor yacht' being reserved for larger power boats.

There are exceptions and borderline cases. For instance, there are quite large sailing boats, such as the twelve-metre racing craft, which are mostly decked over, but have large, open, working cockpits, and they would certainly be regarded as yachts.

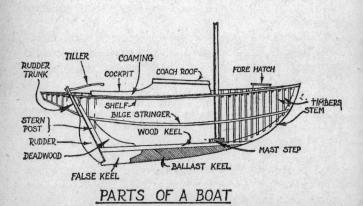

PARTS OF A BOAT

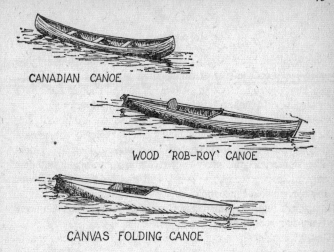

CANADIAN CANOE

WOOD 'ROB-ROY' CANOE

CANVAS FOLDING CANOE

CANOES

The Canadian canoe is the traditional doubled-ended boat which we associate with Red Indians. It is undecked and propelled by a single paddle. They are rarely seen around the coast, being essentially inland waterway craft. Originally built of birch bark, the ones we now see are lightly planked in timber or plywood.

The Rob-Roy canoe is more suitable for rough water, as it is completely decked in, except for a small rectangular cockpit opening. It is built of timber and propelled by a single paddle, but a double-bladed paddle can be used.

The Folboat is a canoe similar to the Rob-Roy type, but it is made of rubberized canvas and can be collapsed and folded away. A flexible cover can be clipped over the cockpit opening, leaving only a body-sized hole which can be tied round the canoeist's waist. Like the Eskimo kayak, of similar design, these canoes can be quite seaworthy. In 1931, the author paddled one from London to Paris, crossing the Channel from coast to coast in about eight hours.

DINGHIES

The smallest boats of all are the one-man inflatable dinghies which formed the seat of pilots' parachutes until required for use in the water. Once in the water, the pilot operated a CO_2 gas cylinder which inflated them within a minute or so. Many were sold for civilian use and they are still seen occasionally.

Inflatable dinghies have now been developed for general marine purposes and make safe and practical yacht tenders. The semi-rigid models powered by medium-sized outboard engines, plane across the water and can hold their own with any conventional speedboat.

Stem dinghies, built of wood and usually of 'clinker' con-

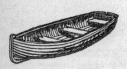 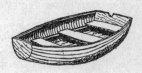

STEM DINGHY   PRAM DINGHY

struction, ie, one plank overlapping the one below it, are the workhorses of the longshoreman, and provide seaworthy yacht tenders for the larger yachts. They can be propelled by oars, outboard engine or sails. When fitted with an inboard engine, the larger ones would be described as motor launches.

When built as a sailing dinghy, they have a centreboard keel which swings down from the middle of the dinghy and offers lateral resistance to the water so that the boat may be sailed into the wind. It would also include, of course, mast, sails and rudder.

The pram dinghy originated in Norway and, although similar to the stem dinghy, has a different-shaped bow. The planking of a stem dinghy is taken to a point and secured to the stem piece, whereas the pram dinghy planking is cut off short and filled in with a small sloping plank, similar to the larger flat transom stern of dinghies. It is a cheaper method of construction and quite suitable for small yacht tenders.

The pram dinghy is also propelled by oars, outboard engine or sometimes by sail. Its keel will usually be in the form of a 'dagger plate', instead of a pivoted centreboard. The 'dagger plate' is a simple flat piece of steel or timber that slides down the centreboard casing. The stem dinghy makes a more seaworthy craft, but the pram dinghy is adequate in sheltered waters.

INSHORE FISHING-BOATS

These boats can be propelled by large outboard engines, but it is more usual to have an inboard engine installed. Ranging from approximately fifteen to thirty feet in length, although they do come larger, they may be open or half-decked, perhaps having a shelter for the helmsman and a small cabin in the forepeak. An essential feature is that they are to all intents and purposes an open boat, or have a large cockpit in which lines, nets and pots can be handled conveniently.

MOTOR CRUISERS

As their name would suggest, these are fully powered boats from about twenty to forty-five feet in length, having cabin accommodation, but no sails or only very small steadying sails and small masts. Larger boats, from forty-five feet in length upwards, would more appropriately be described as motor yachts. They carry no sail, but may have stumpy masts for signal halyards, etc. A hundred-ton motor yacht is considered a large boat these days, and there is no limit to the luxury that can be built into them. One of the largest yachts afloat is the Royal yacht *Britannia* of 5,111 tons.

With building charges what they are today, there is an increasing tendency towards standard designs, which does help to reduce costs. This is in contrast to earlier days when, except for racing-classes, a yacht was a highly individual creation.

BOAT CONSTRUCTION

Wooden hulls can be constructed by any one of several different methods. There is the clinker method already mentioned, usually confined to dinghies and small cruisers, and there is the carvel method, which is normally used for larger boats. In this system, the planking is laid edge to edge, tight on the inside and slightly open on the outside, and secured to frames or timbers which provide the shape of the hull. The narrow 'V' gaps between the planks are caulked by hammering in cotton or oakum, and then filled in flush with putty. After sanding down to a smooth finish, several coats of paint or varnish are applied.

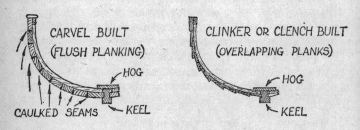

This type of building has the advantage that an old, leaky hull can be recaulked, hardened down, puttied, and is once again as good as new – providing the fastenings are sound. On the other hand, there is not much you can do when a clinker-built boat begins to leak, except patch it with 'tingles', or fit quarter-round beading under the 'lands' of the planking. Carvel construction can be applied to the conventional round bilge or the hard chine hull.

Another method of building a hull is that of double-diagonal planking laid up on light timbers. It is an expensive method which has been used for lifeboats and high-speed service launches, as well as yachts.

Many small boats, such as 'flattie' pram dinghies, speed-boats and small sailing yachts are now built of marine ply-

ROUND-BILGED HULL   HARD-CHINE HULL

wood, using the hard-chine method which favours the use of materials in wide flat sheets.

Vessels approaching a hundred feet in length are built in steel, and as they get larger steel, of course, predominates. More and more sailing and motor yachts, and even offshore fishing-boat hulls, are now being built in glass fibre. Glass-fibre dinghies are now more common than wooden ones. They are watertight, rotproof and impervious to marine worm, but standardization is the price one has to pay for their advantages, as they are mass-produced from a single mould.

Most sailing yachts today have some form of auxiliary power, and it is only the traditionalist who will forgo the comfort and security of having a modern, unobtrusive engine below decks.

A very popular type of cruising yacht is the 'fifty/fifty', which is about as efficient under power as it is under sail, though it might lack the extreme efficiency of the 100-per-cent power or sailing vessel.

SAILING RIGS

The rig of sailing vessels has changed through the ages, partly due to fashion, but mainly because 'sail' has stopped working for its living and has now become the province of the amateur sailor. The square sails of the past were ideal for driving big ships, with big crews, day after day in the constant trade winds of the world, but they are useless in our variable latitudes.

The 'fore-and-aft' rig allows a boat to sail closer into the wind, and is more easily managed. But even with this rig, fashion has changed. In the past, sailing boats in our latitudes favoured the 'gaff' rig, with its short, strong, pole mast, ruggedness and manageability in heavy weather. Damage could be repaired easily with materials on board, and the mast hoops

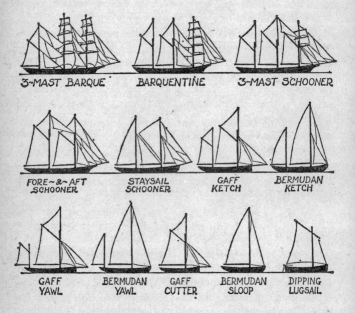

could be used as a ladder to nip up and down the mast when halyards carried away, or when a hand was needed aloft.

With the advent of modern materials, however, the more efficient and easily-handled Bermudan rig has come into its own and has proved itself in long-distance races across the Atlantic Ocean. When someone like Sir Francis Chichester can sail a fifty-foot Bermudan-rigged yacht halfway round the world non-stop, it is difficult to find fault with the rig, but, all the same, its efficiency does depend a lot on good design and strength of materials.

The Bermudan sloop is the simplest of rigs, consisting of a single mast with a tall, narrow triangular mainsail and a large, single foresail. It is the rig for sailing dinghies and small yachts, but the single mainsail becomes rather large and difficult to handle in bigger boats.

For ease of handling in yachts around forty feet or more, the sail plan is often split between two masts, as in the ketch, yawl or schooner. A single-masted vessel carrying two head-sails becomes a cutter instead of a sloop. It might be a Bermudan cutter or a gaff cutter, the latter having a spar called the gaff at the head of the sail, and its second headsail set on a bowsprit. This sail is called the 'jib'. In a ketch, the mainmast (largest) is the forward one, and the mizzenmast (smaller) is aft. But if the mizzenmast is aft of the rudder post, the vessel becomes a yawl.

A schooner usually has two masts, the mainmast being aft. Schooners have been built with six masts, all the same size, but they were large 5,000-ton American sailing ships.

These rigs – as on sloops, gaff and Bermudan cutters, ketches, yawls, schooners, and including 'gunter rig' and 'lug sails' – are all fore-and-aft rigs; the last two usually only being seen on 'knockabout' dinghies, although they were popular rigs on larger boats in bygone days.

A few square-rigged ships are still sailing the oceans of the world, but they are mostly engaged in the sea training of cadets. The only real chance we have of seeing them is during the 'Tall Ships' week, when they congregate from all over the world in the port of Dartmouth in Devon or Falmouth in Cornwall, prior to the start of the Tall Ships Race.

An interesting sailing ship, and one of the largest in Britain, is the *Sir Winston Churchill* which is run by the Sail Training Association for the young people of Britain, and is a regular competitor in the Tall Ships Race. She is a three-masted schooner, 135 feet in length. Her foremast and mainmast are gaff-rigged, and her mizzen is Bermudan, and she also carries a square sail and yard on the foremast. Her two 135 hp diesel engines give her a speed of 9½ knots when she is motoring. She has lately been joined by a near-sister ship, the *Malcolm Miller*. Slightly longer than the *Sir Winston Churchill* at 150 feet overall, this 300-ton topsail schooner was built in Aberdeen and launched in October 1967.

Any young person can apply for a fortnight's cruise on either of these ships and there are no selection boards or examinations to go through. The berths are open to boys of any class, creed, race or colour, and are allotted in order of application. Information about the cruises can be obtained from the Schooner Secretary, The Sail Training Association, Market Chambers, High Street, Petersfield, Hampshire.

SEA SLEDS

The sea sled, which was popular during the 1930s and is now coming into fashion again as a glass-fibre boat, tends to ride on a cushion of air. In this case the V-shaped hull has a certain

SEA SLED

amount of air rammed underneath it by its own forward motion. As the lines of the hull flatten towards the stern, the hull is buoyed up slightly and so planes on the surface.

Sea sleds were designed and patented by a Canadian named Hickman, and well over a hundred were built in various sizes in Britain, most of which were exported to the Canadian lakes. Cabin craft were built up to forty feet in length, and some were fitted with powerful inboard engines with semi-submerged propellers, ie, only the bottom blades being in the water.

The present revival of interest in sea sleds is no doubt because they have several advantages and few disadvantages over more conventional hulls. They have great stability, need very

An aerial view of the Port of London below Tower Bridge showing docks to left and centre

This giant tanker, the motor-ship *Niso*, of 119,378 tons, was built for the Shell Company in Japan in 1966

The 58,000-ton Cunard liner *Queen Elizabeth II*

The offshore drilling rig *Sea Quest*, used to locate sources of natural gas in the bed of the North Sea

Operating a regular service between Southsea and Ryde, this SRN 6 hovercraft carries 38 passengers and is capable of a maximum speed of 55 knots

An older type of yacht, the gaff-rigged ketch *Harebell*, built in 1924.
Of 50 tons TM she measures 70½ ft overall, from bowsprit to end
of counter, and draws 8½ ft

The Sail Training Association's three-masted schooner,
Sir Winston Churchill

An RNLI fast inshore-rescue boat, nearly a hundred of which are located at strategic points round our coasts

A new type of 44-ft steel lifeboat now in service with the RNLI. British-built to an American design, No 44-002 is named *John F. Kennedy*, after the late President of the United States

little water to remain afloat, and can be pushed along with a minimum of power. They can be easily slid over mudflats that have dried out, and on a hard beach can be slipped effortlessly with a roller or two under each side keel.

CATAMARANS

The original catamaran consisted of several logs lashed together and was used on the Indian coast, but the name has also been used to describe canoes fitted with an outrigger, a primitive type of boat used by many races of seamen in warmer latitudes.

The catamarans we see around our coast are twin-hulled

CATAMARAN

motor or sailing craft and, as a class, they have become increasingly popular in recent years. On larger catamarans, the two hulls are joined by continuous decking, forming a fine platform for the crew, and they have great initial stability. However, if forced over on to their beam ends (on their side) they will turn over and stay there. To prevent this some sailing catamarans carry a large round lump of buoyant material at the masthead so that if they do go over they lie flat on the water, instead of turning upside down.

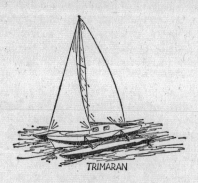

TRIMARAN

TRIMARANS

Trimarans have developed from the catamaran and consist of a normal immersed type of hull, with a subsidiary hull on either side. Both catamarans and trimarans have their enthusiastic adherents, but the conservative seaman still looks a little askance at them.

IMMERSED HULLS

This type of hull floats *in* the water, both at rest and when under way. It is supported by the upward component of the total water pressure action on the immersed portion of the hull. The horizontal component of the water pressure only tends to crush the structure inwards. Flat-bottomed boats that have settled on clay or mud at low water may well refuse to float on the rising tide if the water cannot penetrate under the boat to create an upward pressure on the bottom of the vessel.

Any vessel placed on the surface of a liquid will sink until it has displaced an amount of the liquid equal to its own weight – then it floats at that level. If its weight exceeds the weight of water it can displace – then down it goes to the bottom.

With an immersed hull, it is necessary to streamline the underbody so that it can move reasonably easily through the water. Even so, a wave or wall of water tends to build up in front at the bow, creating a horizontal pressure acting opposite to the direction of motion. This pressure, together with frictional resistance of the water against the hull, has to be exceeded by the power of the engine or sails to achieve any increase in speed.

Not much power is required to move a floating body through the water at slow speed, but once the bow wave begins to form at higher speeds the power required goes up many-fold.

The longer an immersed hull is in relation to its beam, the easier it is to move it through the water for a given amount of propulsive power. Therefore, short-ended, beamy boats are slow by comparison with slim ones, everything else being equal.

Another surprising thing about boats is that whilst an excess of beam gives great stability and a sense of comfort in smooth water, it produces a quick, jerky motion in a rough sea. Its stability in the rolling plane results in the hull maintaining its attitude to the surface of the water, even when the surface water is at a great angle. A less beamy boat, affected relatively more by its keel or ballast than its buoyancy, will lag behind a little, so giving an easier motion in a rolling sea.

PLANING HULL

As there is resistance to moving fast through the water, high-speed boats are designed to plane on the surface of the water, so eliminating the worst effects of the bow wave, and leaving friction and drag as the main retarding forces.

The flat or V-planing hull, although an immersed hull when at rest, gains lift on being propelled forwards, until it is riding

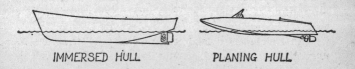

IMMERSED HULL   PLANING HULL

on top of the water and free of the impeding bow wave, subject only to friction and wind resistance. Speed is then limited only by the power available.

But there comes a point when air pressure alone can support the hull, and the boat then becomes an aeroplane and tries to take off, as was the case with Donald Campbell's ill-fated *Bluebird*.

The detail design of planing hulls varies, as will be seen by studying the shape of small speedboats, sea sleds, inboard and outboard motor yachts, RAF tenders and air-sea rescue launches, Naval motor gun boats and torpedo boats – in fact, all boats that get up out of the water and travel fast. Even sailing boats in the small racing classes are designed to plane in strong winds, but not the catamarans – they get their speed by having long, slim, immersed hulls.

Most of the early high-speed hulls were 'stepped', the drag being reduced in stages, as one step after another lifted clear of the water. The hulls of flying boats and seaplanes were often designed like this, but the modern tendency is to have a V-shaped hull with flat lines at the stern.

BOWS AND STERNS

Above the waterline, the design of a ship, yacht or boat depends to a large degree on the use for which she is intended and, to some extent, on fashion.

In the past, the straight stem was popular. There was nothing wrong with it, and it resulted in maximum waterline strength for speed, maximum accommodation, and a nice, easy motion at sea. But with it went the popular, long, overhanging counter stern, which cancelled some of the advantages of the straight stem.

Earlier still, we had the beautiful 'clipper bows', a bequest from the age of the sailing ships that needed an extended bow and bowsprit to carry their headsails. Some designers still favour the clipper bow, and yachts are still being launched with them to this day.

SOME TYPES OF BOW

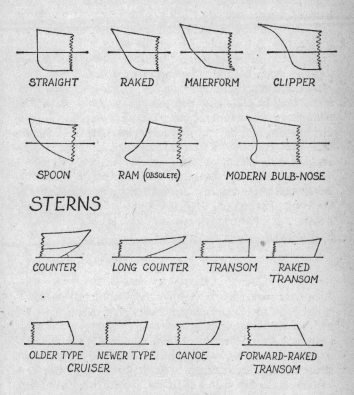

STRAIGHT RAKED MAIERFORM CLIPPER

SPOON RAM (OBSOLETE) MODERN BULB-NOSE

STERNS

COUNTER LONG COUNTER TRANSOM RAKED
TRANSOM

OLDER TYPE NEWER TYPE CANOE FORWARD-RAKED
CRUISER TRANSOM

Big-ship fashion favours the rounded, raked stem, together
with the 'cruiser stern', either raked inwards or outwards. A
type of bow which looks well in big ships is the 'Maierform'
bow, originating from Germany. It is claimed that it im-
proves the speed and behaviour of ships in heavy seas. The
most common bow in modern sailing yachts is the 'spoon' bow,
which is similar to the 'Maierform' bow. It is ideal for the

cruising sailing yacht, but the rounded raked stem is the accepted shape for modern motor yachts.

As already mentioned, little power is required to move an immersed hull through the water up to a certain speed. This speed is determined by multiplying the square root of the waterline length by $1\frac{1}{4}$. Above this speed, a lot more power is required, the bow wave builds up, the stern sinks into a hollow, and there comes a point where any increase of power is useless as it does not add to the vessel's speed.

To prevent the stern sinking in high-speed boats and motor yachts, they are built with wide, flat transom sterns which provide maximum buoyancy. Fast, powerful Naval vessels, such as destroyers, have this square transom stern, as do all speedboats.

Most small pulling dinghies and sailing boats also have transom sterns, but this is chiefly because it is a convenient way of building a boat and provides plenty of buoyancy aft, where it is most needed.

BUYING A BOAT OR YACHT

Buying a small boat of the dinghy class is no more complicated than buying a bicycle – you pay the price asked, get a receipt, and off you go. The purchase of a yacht or motor cruiser, whether new or second-hand is, however, a rather more formal procedure, especially if the yacht is registered as a British ship. Transactions involving second-hand boats are often best handled through a recognized agent, such as a member of the Association of British Yacht Agents. This association is affiliated to the Ship and Boat Builders' National Federation and standard agreement forms for the sale and purchase of yachts are available, which, when completed, protect both vendor and purchaser.

Having taken a fancy to a vessel, the purchaser hands ten per cent of the purchase price to the agent, and then has the boat put ashore and surveyed at his expense. If the survey is satisfactory, the balance of the purchase price is paid against a legal 'bill of sale'. The boat's certificate of registry has then to be sent to the Registrar of Shipping at the Customs House of the port at which the boat is registered, so that the necessary change of ownership can be endorsed upon it.

If, on the other hand, the survey is not acceptable, the agent returns the deposit to the purchaser, and the deal is off.

MARINE SURVEYORS

A yacht or motor cruiser can be a considerable investment, and no one in his senses will normally purchase without obtaining an expert opinion, as one can so easily be blind to obvious faults when it concerns one's 'dreamship'. Any finance house, before lending money for the purchase of a yacht, will require a surveyor's report on the condition of the hull, as will, most likely, the insurance company before issuing a marine policy.

Anyone may carry out a condition survey, providing the purchaser has sufficient confidence in their experience and judgement to employ them, but a survey carried out by an un-qualified surveyor may not be acceptable when applying for a mortgage or insurance.

Professional membership of the Royal Institute of Naval Architects is the usual acceptable qualification, and is de-noted by the letters MRINA or FRINA. The academic qualifications are identical for these chartered Naval architects and surveyors, but transfer from membership to full fellowship is not customarily granted until the candidate has held a responsible position in the industry for a considerable number of years.

Until 1960 there was a non-professional grade of Associate of the Institution, carrying the letters AINA. No academic qualifications were required, and anyone closely asssociated with the marine world, and suitably sponsored, could be con-sidered for election as an Associate of the Institution. This was altered when, in 1960, the centenary year of the Institu-tion, it was granted a Royal Charter and became the Royal Institution of Naval Architects. The right of Associates to add AINA or ARINA after their names was then withdrawn, a ruling which adversely affected a number of marine surveyors who, though they may not have had the necessary academic qualifications, did have a considerable knowledge and experience of boats.

YACHT'S LEVER WINDLASS

CHAPTER EIGHT

Safety at Sea

TRINITY HOUSE AND THE PILOT SERVICE

The Corporation of Trinity House is the authority responsible for the provision and maintenance of all lighthouses and light-ships around the coasts of the British Isles and is also the principal pilotage authority for the United Kingdom.

The first record of Trinity House, so far as is known, is that relating to its incorporation in 1514. In the reign of Elizabeth I, Trinity House acquired its Grant of Arms, and also authority to erect seamarks. And in 1594, the Lord High Admiral surrendered to the Queen the rights of beaconage, buoyage and ballastage vested in him, with the recommendation, which was adopted, that these be bestowed upon Trinity House.

The rights of beaconage included, of course, lighthouses, although a long interval elapsed before the Corporation had all the English lighthouses permanently under its charge, owing to the Crown's practice of issuing patents or grants of lighthouses to private individuals who, on payment of a rent, had the right to collect the dues. These private lights varied in efficiency according to the capacity or rapacity of the owners, and it was not until 1863 that Trinity House was empowered to buy them out. This cost the Corporation, aided by a loan from the State, nearly £1,200,000.

The first lighthouse was built by the Corporation at Lowestoft in 1609, but the most famous is probably the Eddystone, on which site four structures have been built since the seventeenth century, the first three having been under private ownership.

The first light vessel was established on the Nore Sand in 1732 and, despite its frequent drifting, proved so valuable that

end of the century there were five of these in position. With the gradual introduction after 1820 of chain cables in place of hempen ropes, lightships were better able to keep station, and as progress was made with the development of illuminants they became steadily more valuable. Today, with the introduction of radio beacons and automatic forms of fog signalling, they rank among the most important aids to navigation.

The first buoy to be traced in early records is that at the Nore; the date when it was first placed cannot be traced, but in the register it is one of several dating prior to 1684.

The Trinity House history as a pilotage authority took a much more straightforward course. Empowered as the Guild was by Henry VIII after its petition against the admission of ill-qualified and foreign persons as lodesmen in 1604, James I conferred on it powers relating to the compulsory pilotage of shipping, and the exclusive right to license pilots in the River Thames.

The earliest surviving record of a London pilot by name is that of one Ambrose Marshall, who was licensed on February 24th, 1696, to take ships down the river as far as Gravesend.

The Trinity House outport pilotage districts were established by George III in 1808, but it is clear that many of them had existed long before that time. In that year, also, the fee for the renewal of a London pilot's licence was fixed at £3 3s (£3·15); it still remains at that figure.

In 1890, the first steam pilot-cutter was placed on station at Dungeness, and in 1899 Harwich was made the station for North Channel pilots, who had formerly resided as far afield as Yarmouth, Lowestoft, Southwold and Aldeburgh.

A uniform for pilots was first prescribed on May 29th, 1899. Before that it was the custom for Thames pilots to wear silk hats and frock coats.

The Elder Brethren of Trinity House, among whom were leading ship-builders, were frequently consulted by the Crown and the Commissioners of the Navy on various matters such as, for instance, the construction of batteries at Gravesend and Tilbury, but particularly on the design and construction

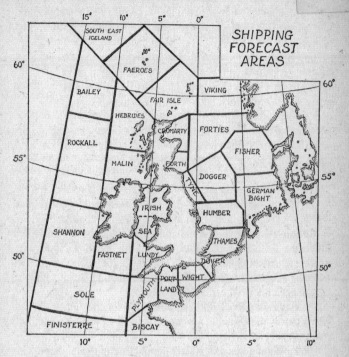

The sea areas used in weather forecasts

of men-of-war. They reported on ships to be purchased and on the proper complements of sailors, armament and stores.

In the seventeenth century, the sphere of the Corporation's activities had become so wide that it would be difficult to discover any maritime matter in which the Brethren did not have some authority or interest. It was their business to erect beacons, to lay buoys, grant certificates to pilots, settle the rate of pilotage, examine and recommend masters for the Navy (until 1874 they examined the officers of the navigation branch, formerly known as masters and mates), and at times to act as an auxiliary press gang. They examined also the mathematical scholars of Christ's Hospital; they appointed British consuls in foreign ports, and had many other duties and powers.

Today, the ten active Elder Brethren comprise nine officers of the Merchant Navy and one of the Royal Navy, one of whom they elect annually as Deputy-Master. These Brethren administer the day-to-day affairs of Trinity House.

The activities with which the Corporation are now empowered to deal are divided into three main functions:

1. As general lighthouse authority for England and Wales, the Channel Islands, with adjacent seas and islands, and Gibraltar.

The Scottish lights are administered by the Northern Lighthouse Commissioners, and the Irish lights, both north and south, by the Irish Light Commissioners. These three General Lighthouse Authorities are financed from the light dues which make up the General Lighthouse Fund. Trinity House has, however, statutory jurisdiction as regards the other two bodies and the Commissioners apply for sanction to Trinity House before erecting or altering any seamark.

2. As the principal pilotage authority for the United Kingdom, being the pilotage authority for the London district and for forty other districts.

The pilotage service is self-supporting, income being derived from licence fees and dues paid by shipowners for the service of pilots.

3. As a charitable organization, it administers certain charitable trusts dedicated to the relief of aged and distressed master mariners, their widows and spinster daughters.

Light dues are payable in respect of all ships over twenty tons, with the exception of HM ships and certain others, such as sailing vessels under 100 tons, ships in ballast without passengers, ships putting in for coal and provisions for their own use, and fishing vessels and ships sheltering.

Trinity House plays a prominent part in 'The International Association of Authorities', which has a permanent secretariat in Paris to organize the five-yearly international conferences and to foster technical cooperation between member countries in every way possible.

A system of remote control covering a group of lighthouses is now being set up in the Holyhead area. In 1966, an off-shore station was brought into the group which sends its signals, and is supervised, by radio link with the Holyhead control centre.

Trinity House is now studying a plan to replace the three lightships around the Goodwin Sands with fixed light-towers. These towers, manned by a crew of three instead of the seven at present on the lightships, would be provided with helicopter landing-decks and would eventually be made fully automatic.

In terms of the mariners' safety, the demand has always been for maximum efficiency and reliability, which is why the work of Trinity House has, from the beginning, been administered by a board of experienced sailors. The ultimate responsibility for its efficient operation rests with each individual, ashore and afloat – from the Elder Brother laying off the arc of a light to the pilot guiding a great ship to her port; or the light-house-keeper on his lonely watch – each is a vital link in the Trinity House chain of service to the mariner.

TRINITY HOUSE SHIP

The Trinity House committee ship is the *Patricia*, a smart black and white vessel whose duty it is to carry out inspections and servicing of the lightships and buoyage system which come under Trinity House jurisdiction. Other tenders are also engaged in the servicing of offshore lighthouses, lightships and buoys, from depots strategically positioned around our coast.

The Trinity House vessel *Winston Churchill*, commissioned in May 1963, is the latest Trinity House tender and one of four similar vessels built since 1959. The others are *Mermaid*, *Siren* and *Stella*.

LIGHT VESSELS

Whilst lighted buoys are used to warn shipping of dangerous shoals and rocks, and to mark out deep-water channels, major hazards to the mariner which cannot be marked by a fixed structure often warrant the powerful warning light of a lightship.

In 1732 a primitive lightship, burning candles in a lantern, was moored with hemp cables on the Nore Sand, and by the end of the century four more were in use, including one on the Goodwin Sands. In 1820, special vessels were being built, and chain cables replaced hemp rope.

LIGHT VESSEL

Today, steel lightships are on station around our shores, carrying a powerful light forty feet above the water, with a characteristic flash by which it can be identified. They are equipped with powerful fog signals and some are fitted with radio beacons as a guide for ships equipped with direction-finding apparatus.

To ensure that the beam of the powerful electric light remains horizontal in rough weather when the lightship is rolling badly, the apparatus is pendulum-balanced and swung in gimbals.

Although they have generators to produce electricity for the lantern, fog signals, radio and domestic lighting, light vessels have no propulsive machinery and have to be towed to and from their stations.

The most modern type of British light vessel is 133 feet in length and has a beam of twenty-six feet. The crew consists of a master and two seamen, two fog-signal drivers and two lamplighters. Their tour of duty lasts one month. Lightships are painted red, and have the name of the station painted in large white letters along each side of the hull.

THE LIFEBOAT SERVICE

The Lifeboat Institution was founded in 1824, but there were lifeboats in service even before that time. Many were provided by Lloyd's, others by private individuals, but there was no proper coordination and funds were limited.

Controlled by the Royal National Lifeboat Institution, which provides and maintains lifeboats in the United Kingdom and the Irish Republic, and supported entirely by voluntary contributions, the service's sole purpose is to rescue life at sea.

There are 150 lifeboats stationed around the 5,000-mile-long coastline of Great Britain and Ireland, and they have rescued over 87,000 people since 1824.

The usual arrangement is that there is one full-time member of the crew at each station, and he is the motor mechanic. The coxswain, second coxswain and bowman, who are known as 'boat's officers', receive small retaining fees, and all members of the crew are paid rewards by the hour whenever they go out on service or exercise.

It is not generally known but, apart from the saving of life for which no charge is made, the crew may use the lifeboat to salvage any craft, and they are then entitled to claim salvage money and share it amongst themselves. The money does not go to the Royal National Lifeboat Institution. Yachtsmen should, therefore, think twice before asking for or accepting a tow as a convenience, when they are not in any real danger, or they may find themselves saddled with a salvage claim.

There are normally eight men in the lifeboat's crew, four of them being the 'boat's officers' and motor mechanic, together with an assistant motor mechanic and three deckhands, some of whom are qualified in first-aid or as radio operators or signalmen. Smaller boats have a crew of only seven.

A lifeboat can either be launched down a slipway direct from a boathouse or be taken to the sea on a carriage towed by a waterproofed tractor. Some lifeboats are permanently moored afloat in harbours or estuaries; others are launched down a beach on skids.

Apart from the normal items needed for navigation, their equipment includes radio telephone on shipping and aircraft wavebands, loudhailers, searchlights, signalling lamps, line-throwing pistols, direction-finding radio, echo-sounding gear, together with oil for rough seas, stretchers, blankets, axes, flares, and suchlike.

In an average year, lifeboats launch most frequently to fishing-boats, yachts accounting for the second highest number of service calls. Lifeboats are called upon to perform a variety of different services, including the landing of sick people from remote islands, taking doctors out to ships, and rescuing people who have been cut off by the tide at the bottom of cliffs.

Lifeboats vary in size and in certain other respects according to launching conditions. There are now two standard types of lifeboat being built, both of which will right themselves automatically if they capsize. These are the 48½-foot and 37-foot Oakley lifeboats, both of which have wooden hulls. Experiments have been carried out with a 44-foot steel lifeboat which was obtained from the United States Coast Guard to enable the Royal National Lifeboat Institution to decide whether to build similar boats in this country.

During 1965–6, the new 70-foot steel lifeboats, designed for offshore rescue work, went into service, the first one being stationed in the approaches to the Bristol Channel, usually under the lee of Lundy Island. They are manned by full-time crews and commanded by coxswains holding a master mariner's certificate. Each tour of duty lasts fourteen days.

The lifeboat's hull incorporates six watertight bulkheads, and in the engine room a bulkhead running fore and aft forms a separate engine room for each of the two 220-hp Gardner diesel engines. These 70-foot lifeboats carry two inflatable rescue dinghies, one with a 33-hp outboard engine, and one with an 18-hp engine. These fast, inflatable rescue boats are also being widely used on inshore rescue service. There are now upwards of a hundred positioned around our coasts and, being capable of 20 knots and quickly launched, they can deal with minor operations more efficiently than the traditional lifeboat.

A list of stations, arranged geographically round the coastline, at which RNLI lifeboats may be seen will be found in an appendix at the back of this book.

CHAPTER NINE

A Ship's Equipment

ROPE

We all know what rope is – or do we?

Until recent times, all rope was made up from short natural fibres of hemp, manila, cotton, sisal or coir, twisted together, usually right-handed, into a continuous length of yarn. Several yarns are then taken and twisted together to form left-handed strands. Then three strands are twisted right-handed to form a hawser – 'laid rope', as we know it. Sometimes, four strands are twisted together to form a hawser but, size for size, the three-stranded rope is the strongest.

For special purposes rope is 'laid up' in the opposite direction, the final twist being left-handed, and we then have 'left-handed' rope. Never join a length of left-handed rope to a length of right-handed rope, as any strain on it will tend to untwist the 'lay'.

When new rope is being taken from the coil, it is better to take it from the middle, and uncoil it anti-clockwise if it is right-handed rope, as it will not then kink so badly in use. It is important to be able to determine which is right-handed and which is left-handed rope. Holding the rope straight out from you, note which way the strands run. The rope is right-handed if it starts from the left and runs away from you to the right.

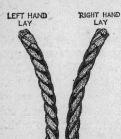

LEFT HAND LAY   RIGHT HAND LAY

When coiling down right-handed rope, it must be coiled down clockwise, otherwise it will become kinky and un-usable. New rope will always tend to be kinky and before use it is wise to stretch it out and take out the turns, or tow it behind a boat for a while.

Cable-laid rope consists of three right-handed hawsers twisted together left-handed. It is this type of rope that was used to anchor ships before chain cable came into use.

Ropes made of natural fibres are rapidly being replaced by 'man-made' fibres, examples of which are nylon and terylene, although there are many others. Terylene is a polyester filament derived from oil, and nylon is a polyamide filament made from oil and coal. Unlike natural fibres which come in varying short lengths, these filaments are continuous, which accounts for their much greater strength.

As terylene does not stretch, it is used as halyards in the rigging of sailing vessels, and in the manufacture of the sails themselves. Nylon, on the other hand, will stretch twenty per cent in length and absorb shock loads four times greater than wire rope of the same size. For this reason it is particularly suitable for use as warps, moorings, tow ropes, etc.

WARPS

When vessels are berthed alongside a quay wall, the ropes they are made fast with are called 'warps'. To prevent the ship ranging about and to keep her parallel to the quay, a recognized pattern of warps are run ashore and secured to bollards. We have 'breast ropes' at bow and stern to keep her straight, and 'for'ard springs' and 'back springs' to prevent any movement up and down the quay.

RIGGING

Any rope used in the rigging of a vessel has its own particular name. Those which hoist sails are called 'halyards' as are also the lighter lines that hoist flags, burgees, etc. The ropes that control the angle of the sail in relation to the wind are 'sheets'; thus we have mainsail sheets, jib sheets, foresail sheets and so on. The rope that supports the boom when no sail is set is the 'topping lift', and then there are 'shrouds' and 'stays' which hold a spar or boom in position.

The 'standing rigging', ie, the permanent rigging that supports the masts, bowsprit, etc, is usually of wire rope. The thwartships wire ropes that support the mast and the bowsprit are called 'shrouds', and the fore-and-aft wire ropes are called 'stays'. Lines secured horizontally from forward shroud to after shroud on the same side of the ship are known as 'ratlines'. They form a means of access to the 'hounds', that part of the mast from which the upper ends of the shrouds are secured. When a ship is moored to a buoy, a rope passed from the bowsprit end to the buoy, to prevent the buoy bumping the bows, is called a 'bull rope'.

BERTHING

When a vessel approaches a quay wall with the intention of berthing alongside, one line is heaved ashore from the bows and another from the stern. This is a special light 'heaving

THE HEAVING LINE

'NIGGERHEAD' BOLLARD

Heaving lines are used to drag warps ashore, where they are secured to bollards or mooring posts

line' kept for the purpose, one end of which has a 'manrope' knot worked into it to give it some weight when being thrown or 'heaved' ashore in a wind. The inboard end is 'bent' (tied) to a heavier mooring warp or wire.

Some handy person ashore – it might be you – catches the heaving line and hauls ashore the warp or wire, which will probably have a large eye or loop spliced in the end. This loop

SHROUDS – OLD STYLE AND NEW

Serving as lateral stays to a
mast, shrouds are usually
of wire and could be
climbed by means
of footropes,
known as
ratlines

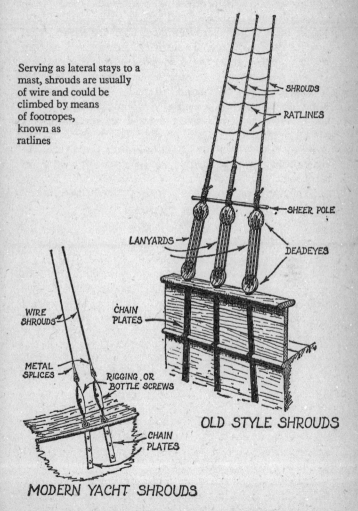

SHROUDS

RATLINES

SHEER POLE

LANYARDS

DEADEYES

WIRE
SHROUDS

CHAIN
PLATES

METAL
SPLICES

RIGGING OR
BOTTLE SCREWS

CHAIN
PLATES

OLD STYLE SHROUDS

MODERN YACHT SHROUDS

is smartly dropped over the most convenient bollard or samson post, the hands on board then take in the slack and, with a turn or two around the warping drum of a windlass, warp the ship into her berth. If there is no loop in the end of the warp, it is passed round the bollard and belayed with several 'figure-of-eight' turns if the bollard is of the double 'niggerhead' type; or two or three turns round a single bollard or post, and then hitched a couple of times on the 'standing part'.

It is very satisfying to be able to cast a heaving line neatly and accurately for a considerable distance. You first of all coil up the line so that it lays naturally, without any tendency to kink. Then you take the heaving end and half the coil in your right hand, holding the other half of the coil securely with the left hand. With a swinging action, heave the first half of the coil, allowing the second half to run out of the left hand as required.

CHAIN CABLE

The size of a rope or wire is the measure of its circumference in inches. The size of chain on the other hand, is the diameter of the bar from which the individual links are made.

Chain has an advantage over rope and wire, when used as an anchor cable, in possessing a considerable weight of its own which reduces dangerous 'snubbing' or snatching when a vessel is pitching in a seaway. The weight of the chain ensures that a

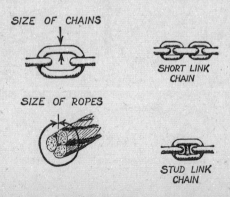

SIZE OF CHAINS

SHORT LINK CHAIN

SIZE OF ROPES

STUD LINK CHAIN

length of it lies on the bottom as it runs away from the anchor to the ship, and this has to be lifted bar tight before the vessel snubs. Another advantage is that this length of chain on the bottom increases the holding power of the anchor.

Chain cable is manufactured with plain links or with links having a bar, or stud, across the middle of the link. The latter is called 'studded-link' chain, the stud preventing distortion of the link when subjected to a great strain. Surprisingly enough, studded-link chain has a tensile strength less than that of open-link chain.

ANCHORS

Big ships use stockless anchors which can be stowed in the hawsepipe, instead of having to stow them inboard, on deck – quite a consideration when handling anchors of around ten tons in weight.

Small working boats and large yachts, on which it would be difficult to manhandle anchors aboard, usually have a 'cat davit' right in the eyes of the boat. As the anchor breaks the surface, a tackle is hooked into the ring of the balancing band

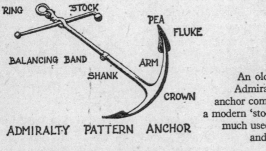

RING   STOCK   PEA   FLUKE

BALANCING BAND   ARM

SHANK   CROWN

ADMIRALTY PATTERN ANCHOR

An old-fashioned Admiralty-pattern anchor compared with a modern 'stockless' type much used by yachts and small craft

'CQR' ANCHOR

midway up the shank so that it can be hauled up over the rail and stowed on deck.

The holding power of a stockless anchor, as used by big ships, depends mainly on its own weight but, for smaller boats, light, stockless anchors of the Danforth or CQR type have excellent holding power, having been so designed that they tend to bury themselves in the sea bed.

The old-fashioned but well-proven anchors of the 'fisherman' type, and the Admiralty and the Nicholson patterns, depend on the 'stock' to keep the fluke of the anchor biting into the bottom.

WINDLASSES

The windlass is an essential piece of equipment when the size and weight of chain and anchor are too great for manhandling. It consists of rope-warping drums and a chain gipsy, with a

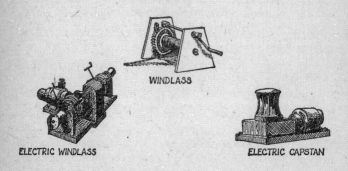

WINDLASS

ELECTRIC WINDLASS

ELECTRIC CAPSTAN

clutch between them so that they may be worked independently. Windlasses can be powered by steam, electricity, or hydraulically operated from the main engines. On small boats and yachts they are more often geared down and manually operated by handles or levers.

Windlasses of olden days, which may still be seen on old fishing-boats such as the East Coast 'bawleys', take the form of a wooden drum, with 'dogs' or strips of raised metal on it to grip the rope and reduce wear. The wooden drum is supported horizontally between vertical stout timbers, and is installed athwartships on the foredeck. The drum is rotated by the leverage of wooden timbers which are inserted in holes at either end of the drum. It was a primitive and inconvenient arrangement, as the chain could not be cast off for quick manhandling when there was slack to be got rid of. Consequently, as it built up on one section of the drum, a trick of 'flaking' it along the drum had to be resorted to.

CAPSTAN

The more familiar, old-fashioned capstan, still used ashore and afloat, was more practical, though it was not so strong since it revolved on a vertical axle and was supported only at the bottom end. However, as it revolved in the horizontal plane, propelled by capstan bars inserted in holes at the top, the crew could heave away steadily to the chant of sea shanties, such as *Whisky Johnny* or *Blow the Man Down*. It also had the advantage that the warp or cable could be cast off the drum as necessary.

WINCHES

The winch is a similar piece of equipment to the windlass, but it handles wire and sometimes rope, but not chain cable. Winches are sited on deck to give a convenient run for the wires of the cargo derricks. They are always powered on ships, usually by steam. Modern sailing yachts have small ratchet winches with detachable handles, and these are mounted on the mast and in the cockpit to facilitate the handling of halyards and sheets. In use, two or three turns of wire or rope on the revolving drums are sufficient to take the load, the friction being maintained by the operator as he leads the line off. He only has to let the line go slack, and can then slip the load to suit himself.

CRANES

A crane is a lifting device which does the same job as a derrick or sheer legs, but has its own integral power unit and winding drum, with sufficient wire for its operational lift. Some modern cargo ships have level-luffing cranes to handle cargo, instead of the usual cargo derrick powered by separate winches.

BOLLARDS

A rope, be it halyard, sheet or warp, would be useless at sea or ashore, without a good, strong anchorage on which to make it fast. The single or double bollard, made of metal and well secured to the ground or deck, is probably the most common form of anchorage. Samson posts serve the same purpose as a

CLEATS

BOLLARDS

single bollard, but usually take the form of a stout, vertical piece of timber, well secured through the deck and down to the keel. Alternatively, on shore, it might be a timber pile extended a few feet above its neighbours in the structure of a pier.

CLEATS

These are of wood or metal, usually in hard wood or yellow metal on yachts, but, on a working ship, they may only be a short length of round steel bar welded to a stanchion or rail. The cleat is secured so that the pull of the rope comes in the lengthwise direction of the cleat itself. The line is given one round turn around the cleat and then belayed with two or three figures-of-eight. A belayed rope can always be cast off quickly, as there is no danger of the rope jamming.

BITTS

These are strong upright posts secured through the deck to frames, with a stout crosspiece joining them a little below the top of the uprights. They may form the inboard anchorage for

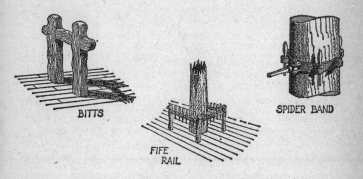

BITTS

FIFE RAIL

SPIDER BAND

the end of a bowsprit, in which case they are ideal for belaying the anchor cable. When mounted on deck at the mast, they can be used for the securing and belaying halyards.

FIFE RAIL

This is a horizontal piece of wood or metal having several holes to take belaying pins. Any line or halyard is then belayed vertically over the pins.

SPIDER BAND

This is another anchorage for halyards, etc, but is mounted around the mast and has lugs formed on it to take belaying pins. It may also include a lug to support the 'gooseneck' fitting of a boom end.

BELAYING PIN

BELAYING PIN

A vertical pin through a horizontal rail. They are usually loose, having a collar which prevents them dropping right through the hole. In the days of big sailing ships, when all the gear was much heavier than it is today, a belaying pin provided a handy weapon to crack the skull of the opposition.

TACKLE

Pronounced 'taykle', this is a combination of pulley blocks with rope or chain to form a 'purchase' – a device that will multiply the force available, but at the expense of movement. There are many variations of 'tackle' to be seen around ships and harbours, for use whenever a load has to be lifted by man-power. The pulley block may be of wood, metal, or fibre-reinforced plastic, and comprises a shell with one or more revolving sheaves. The mechanical advantage obtained is proportional to the number of sheaves in the moving block.

HATCHES

These vary in type from the old timber hatch covers, which are manhandled in smaller boats and slung by means of der-

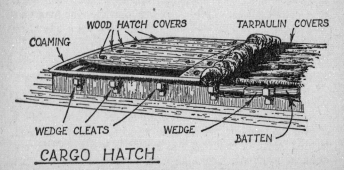

CARGO HATCH

ricks and deck winches in larger vessels, to the modern, steel, folding hatches with their own power and cranes.

At sea, the traditional timber hatches are covered by tarpaulins and secured round the hatch coaming with wooden wedges. The tarpaulins, usually more than one, render the hatches watertight and any seas breaking on board run off harmlessly through the 'scuppers' – holes in the bulwarks at deck level.

FAIRLEADS

As their name suggests, these lead warps and suchlike clear any part of the structure that may tend to 'chafe' the rope. They

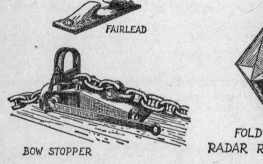

FAIRLEAD

BOW STOPPER

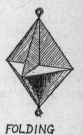

FOLDING
RADAR REFLECTOR

are usually made of metal, open at the top wide enough for the rope to drop in easily, but not so wide that the rope jumps out as the ship ranges about. The internal curves are smooth to reduce friction.

CHAIN STOPPER

This is a heavy metal casting through which the anchor cable is led, positioned between the windlass and the hawsepipe. A lever is incorporated which forces a cam down on to the chain so that it can be controlled as it runs out when anchoring. Without some such device an anchor cable can be a menace

BLOCKS AND PURCHASES

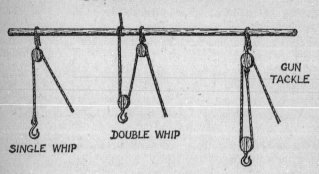

SINGLE WHIP

DOUBLE WHIP

GUN TACKLE

PARTS OF A BLOCK

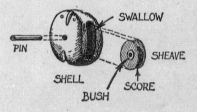

SWALLOW

PIN

SHEAVE

SHELL

SCORE

BUSH

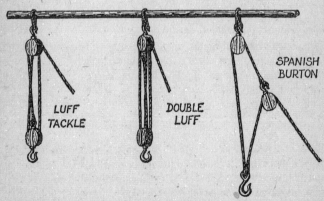

LUFF TACKLE

DOUBLE LUFF

SPANISH BURTON

Various types of tackle used for lifting loads by manpower

and is best kept clear of, even in quite small yachts. There are different patterns, such as 'bow stoppers' and 'chain pipe stoppers', but the principle is the same in each case.

RADAR SCANNERS

Up above the bridge of big ships, or on top of the deckhouse on large yachts and work boats, can be seen the post-war 'with it' status symbol – the radar scanner. It sends out a burst of radio energy and collects the radio echo that rebounds from any object, recording its direction and distance as a visual display on a screen similar to a domestic television screen. As the scanner is constantly rotating, it covers all areas round the ship.

RADAR REFLECTOR

As wooden vessels and small objects low down in the water, such as navigational buoys, do not reflect back a very good echo to ships equipped with radar installations, special radar reflectors are fitted. They are usually made of sheet aluminium in the shape of a diamond, providing multiple reflecting surfaces at different angles. They are remarkably effective and should be carried by all small wooden boats that might find themselves in the track of shipping with the risk of being run down at night or in conditions of poor visibility.

DF RADIO

On many ships and yachts, again high on the bridge or deckhouse, will be seen a hoop-shaped object, supported on one edge by a vertical spindle, so that it can be rotated through 360 degrees.

This is a loop aerial which, because of its shape, becomes directional. The maximum signal is received by a loop aerial when the loop is edgewise on to the transmitting station, and the minimum signal when it is flat on to the station. The maximum signal is not well defined, but the minimum signal gives a sharp 'null' over a small angular movement of the rotating aerial. The direction of the station is then at right-angles to the plane of the loop.

Special, long-wave, low-powered transmitters broadcast their identifying signal from known coastal positions all over the world. There are eighty of these DF stations around the

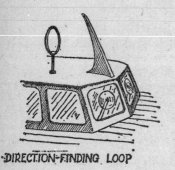

DIRECTION-FINDING LOOP

RADAR SCANNER
(MOUNTED ON CROSSTREE)

coast of Britain alone. Most of them operate continuously, but a few broadcast only during conditions of low visibility. These stations can be heard transmitting their morse identifying signal, together with a long tuning dash of twenty-five seconds, around the 1,000-metre end of the long-wave band on domestic radio receivers.

PATENT LOG

Right on the stern rail of a ship, boat or yacht, may often be seen a small instrument with a clock face, several small hands and a dial calibrated in nautical miles. This is a patent log, which measures the distance the vessel travels through the water.

Once clear of the harbour, a long plaited line with a metal rotor on the outboard end is streamed out aft, and the inboard end hooked on to the recording instrument. As the rotor is drawn through the water it turns the line, which rotates the geared mechanism and registers the distance travelled.

When the log line and rotor are brought back inboard, the drill is to unhook the line off the rotor and pay out the hook end of the line as the rotor comes in. Once the rotor is aboard, you can then haul the line in without producing a snarled up tangle of line impossible to sort out. The uninitiated rarely make the mistake twice.

ROTATOR

ALL LINES ARE PLAITED ROPE

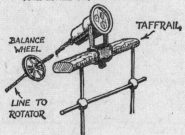

THE PATENT LOG

KNOT (Nautical Mile)

The nautical mile of 6,080 feet is slightly longer than the statute mile of 5,280 feet. When it is said that a ship is doing twenty knots, it means that she is covering twenty nautical miles per hour – one never says 'twenty knots per hour', which would be like saying 'twenty nautical miles per hour per hour'.

The standard for the nautical mile is based on the distance measured along a meridian of one minute of latitude, so that one degree of latitude is equivalent to sixty nautical miles. The nautical or sea mile is sub-divided into ten cables, so that one cable equals, very nearly, 200 yards. The 'league' of olden days is equivalent to three nautical miles.

DRAFT MARKS

Under the Merchant Shipping Act, seagoing vessels, with the exception of certain classes such as yachts, pilot vessels, and lifeboats, are required to have draft marks on their stem and stern posts. These then show at a glance what depth of water is required to float them.

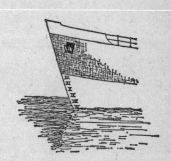

The draft marks on the stem of this ship show she is drawing seven feet of water

LOAD LINE

It is also required by law that every merchant ship shall have a 'load line' marked on each side of the vessel, which must not be submerged when afloat in smooth water. This is a safeguard against overloading.

The load line is known as the Plimsoll Line, as it was Samuel Plimsoll who, in 1876, introduced the Merchant Shipping Act that made the overloading of ships illegal.

A single load line is not sufficient, as the density, and therefore the buoyancy, of water varies with its salinity and temperature. Also, there are varying weather conditions to consider during different seasons of the year. So, instead of a single load line, we see an intriguing pattern of marks painted on a ship's side indicating the maximum draft to which a ship may be laden for any particular voyage.

There are several assigning authorities responsible for the

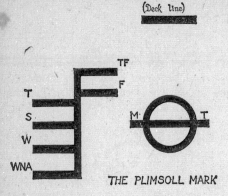

(Deck line)

The horizontal line
bisecting the circle
indicates the ship's
summer load line
in salt water

THE PLIMSOLL MARK

location of load lines on merchant ships, such as the Ministry
of Transport, Lloyd's Register, Bureau Veritas, and American
Bureau – indicated by the letters 'MT', 'LR', 'BV', and 'AB'.
These letters are to be found one on each side of the disc. The
horizontal line across the middle of the disc indicates the summer load line in salt water.

The additional load lines are: T (Tropical); S (Summer);
W (Winter); WNA (Winter North Atlantic); TF (Tropical
Fresh); and F (Fresh Water).

SWINGING THE LEAD

Standing by the rail amidships, the leadsman swings the lead
well forward so that it has time to sink to the bottom by the
time the lead line is 'up and down' or vertical. If the depth
happens to correspond with the piece of red bunting, the leadsman then sings out 'By the mark, seven'. But if the water level
came just between the white calico rag and red bunting, his
cry would then be, 'The deep six'. The word 'by' is always
omitted when calling the 'deeps'.

Intermediate depths would be indicated to the nearest
quarter fathom as follows:

'And a quarter five	–	$5\frac{1}{4}$ fathoms
'And a half five'	–	$5\frac{1}{2}$ fathoms
'Less a quarter six'	–	$5\frac{3}{4}$ fathoms

For deep-sea soundings, a deep sea lead (pronounced 'dipsey') is used with a heavier weight of 28 pounds and a line of 120 fathoms. In this case, the vessel is stopped, and several hands take coils of the line, each one calling out 'Watch there, watch' as his coil runs off. An officer takes the final sounding when the line is up and down.

LEAD LINE

The old-fashioned 'lead line' may still be seen coiled and hitched to the rail of small vessels and yachts. It consists of a line, something over 20 fathoms long (1 fathom equals 6 feet), with a seven-pound lead 'bent' or tied on the end. The bottom end of the lead is hollowed out so that it can be 'armed' with tallow or soap. A sample of the bottom adheres to the tallow, and this itself is an aid to navigation, as the seaman's chart indicates the type of bottom to be found, as well as giving the soundings in fathoms.

At intervals from the lead, the line is marked as follows:

At 2 fathoms		Piece of leather with two tails
3	”	Piece of leather with three tails
5	”	Piece of white calico
7	”	Red bunting
10	”	Piece of leather with a hole in it
13	”	Piece of blue cloth
15	”	Piece of white calico
17	”	Red bunting
20	”	Cord with two knots in it

All the above numbers are called 'marks', and the unmarked fathoms are called 'deeps'.

THE LEAD LINE

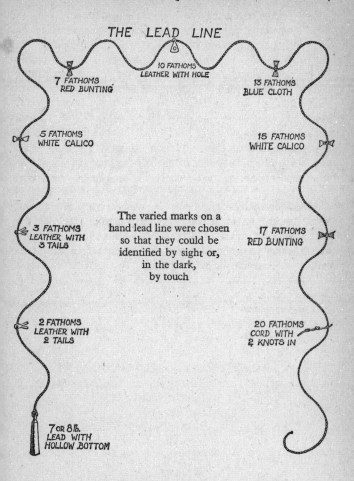

10 FATHOMS
LEATHER WITH HOLE

7 FATHOMS
RED BUNTING

13 FATHOMS
BLUE CLOTH

5 FATHOMS
WHITE CALICO

15 FATHOMS
WHITE CALICO

3 FATHOMS
LEATHER WITH
3 TAILS

The varied marks on a
hand lead line were chosen
so that they could be
identified by sight or,
in the dark,
by touch

17 FATHOMS
RED BUNTING

2 FATHOMS
LEATHER WITH
2 TAILS

20 FATHOMS
CORD WITH
2 KNOTS IN

7 OR 8 lb.
LEAD WITH
HOLLOW BOTTOM

PATENT SOUNDING MACHINE

The sounding machine, mounted on deck near the rail, incorporates a winding drum to feed out and recover a thin wire,
on the end of which there is a weighted brass container holding an open-ended glass tube, the inside of which has been

treated with chromate of silver. With the open end of the glass tube downwards, the increasing pressure of the water as the weighted container sinks deeper and deeper forces water up the tube discolouring the silver chromate to the calibrated depth on the glass. This method allows deep soundings to be taken without completely stopping the ship.

ECHO SOUNDER

All large vessels and many pleasure boats and fishing-boats, now boast an echo sounder of one type or another. This is an electronic apparatus that bounces a high-frequency sound wave from a transducer secured to the bottom of the hull down to the sea bed and back up to the transducer. It measures the time interval and converts it into depth, which is registered as a point of light on a calibrated dial. A more sophisticated model records the depth and a contour of the sea bed on a continuous strip of paper.

CHAPTER TEN

Navigation and Seamanship

NAVIGATING THE SEAS

Navigation as an art can be a very intricate subject indeed, but navigation as practised by most of us at sea is comparatively simple. It can be divided into two parts, coastal navigation and deep-sea navigation. Of the two, the former is the more important, and anyone intending to venture beyond the harbour entrance should get hold of one of the many books devoted to coastal navigation.

Coastal navigation is largely a matter of common-sense – from your charts you determine the bearing of the point you wish to reach and convert this into a compass course, or course to be steered, by applying 'variation' for the area and 'deviation' according to the given course. Tides, currents and wind effect (leeway) have also to be allowed for and while under way positions are checked and confirmed by compass bearings of prominent objects ashore, or by using a sextant to ascertain, by angular measurement, the distance off from a lighthouse. The taking of 'soundings' is another important part of coastal navigation, as the contour of the sea bed is shown on the charts, and it provides a check on position.

Coastal navigation can be of fascinating interest and no one should assume that it is beyond his mental capacity or that there is any need to be an expert mathematician. The most important thing to remember is to have confidence in your own navigation. Having laid down courses to steer, stick to them; do not edge off one way or the other because you feel you should be over 'thataway' a little. Directional 'instincts' in navigation are more often wrong than right.

Deep-sea navigation might appear to be a much more complex subject than coastal navigation, but it need not be, using the modern 'short table' method. The navigator out in the ocean chooses a convenient position and assumes for the moment that his ship is in that position. His tables tell him that the sun, the moon, or a certain star, is at a given altitude above the horizon for that position at that moment. However, his position was only a guess, so he measures the actual altitude (angle in degrees) with his sextant, and finds out what the difference is. Knowing the difference, he can then determine how far he is away from his assumed position and lay the correct position on the chart – and there you are. Perhaps there is a little more to it than that, but not enough to deter anyone of ordinary intelligence.

A simple form of astro-navigation can be practised without tables or instruments, and Columbus and the early Arabian and Polynesian navigators all used such methods. To them, the starry heavens were considered as the mirror of the oceans, marked off by fixed white beacons more efficiently than any light and buoyage system of man's invention.

Many centuries before Columbus, deep-sea navigators were finding their way across the Pacific Ocean by the overhead star method. They knew from their own observations, and those of their forefathers, that particular stars always passed over certain islands. This would give them their approximate position, and to make a landfall they watched the flight of birds, or looked for the reflection of an island against a blue sky, or any of the other natural indications of land.

In the northern hemisphere no one goes to sea without the means of determining his latitude, for he has been blessed with a fixed shining beacon in the shape of the Pole Star which marks the projected pole of the earth against the night sky. It is only necessary to measure the angle between the horizon and the Pole Star with a sextant and the answer, in degrees and minutes, is your latitude.

Early Arabian navigators used this method, and they only had their outstretched fingers held at arms' length with which to measure the required angle – a method which is more accurate than one would expect.

THE POLE STAR 'CLOCK'

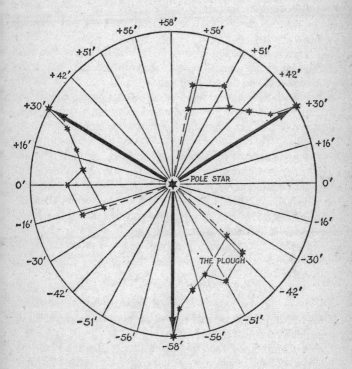

The Pole Star is not exactly over the North Pole, but makes a small circle of one degree around it, so that a simple correction from tables has to be applied to obtain one's precise latitude. But even without the correction, the maximum error can only be sixty miles.

Alternatively, the degree of error can be ascertained without using tables by noting the position in the sky of the well-known pattern of stars we call the 'Plough'. Together with all the other stars, the 'Plough' circles around the Pole Star, and if you join an imaginary line from the end star of the 'Plough's' handle to the Pole Star and think of it as the hands of a clock, then when the hand is at twelve o'clock you must add one degree to the angle of the Pole Star to obtain your latitude. At three and nine o'clock there is no correction to apply, and at six o'clock you subtract one whole degree to obtain the correct latitude.

The correction to apply to the observed altitude, when the 'Plough' is at intermediate positions can be estimated or read off the diagram on the previous page.

If good judgement is shown when estimating the correction to apply, the latitude found should be correct to within five minutes, or five nautical miles – accurate enough to make any landfall.

A marine sextant for measuring altitudes can only be used when there is a visible horizon, so a Pole Star sight may often only be possible at morning and evening twilight. With the ex-RAF Mk IX bubble sextant, which can be bought cheaply from ex-Service stores, observations can be taken throughout the night on land or sea, and although it is not as accurate as a marine sextant, given plenty of practice in its use, it is reliable enough.

THE MAGNETIC COMPASS

The magnetic compass is accepted with little thought these days, which is not altogether surprising since it was the earliest scientific instrument devised by man.

The Chinese and the Phoenicians knew about magnetism thousands of years ago, the name being a derivative of Magnesia, a province of Asia Minor and the source of an iron ore with strong magnetic properties.

This iron ore, or lodestone, when hung freely on a strand of silk was found always to settle in a constant direction – and man was on his way to being a navigator.

Any freely-suspended magnet is affected by the earth, as the earth itself is a large magnet. As 'like' poles of two magnets repel each other, and as 'unlike' poles attract, so the north-seeking end of a magnetic needle will point to the north magnetic pole of the earth. It follows then that the pointer on a compass needle must be the south pole of the magnetic needle, though we think of it as north because it points to the north.

VARIATION

Unfortunately, the north magnetic pole of the earth is not located at the true North Pole, but is a thousand miles away in the north of Canada. This error, measured in degrees, varies in relation to any position on the earth's surface and is known as the 'variation'. Navigational charts show the variation for the particular area they cover, so that the navigator can allow for it when calculating his course to steer by compass.

DEVIATION

In the days of wooden ships, compass correction was no great problem, but as iron and steel came into use afloat complications arose, as these metals become magnetized and can affect the compass needle. For this reason, a second correction for an error known as 'deviation' has also to be applied when working out a compass course.

Deviation is not constant but varies with the direction of the ship's head, angle of heel, change of cargo, switching on and off any electrical circuits, not to mention the changing value of sub-permanent magnetism in the ship's hull.

It is an interesting fact that whilst a ship is being built on the stocks and pointing in one direction relative to the north magnetic pole, the constant hammering and riveting sets up a sub-permanent magnetic force in her structure. After launching, the ship is turned in the opposite direction whilst in the fitting-out dock, where further hammering can cancel some of it out again.

On small vessels and yachts, a deviation correction card is prepared, showing the compass deviation on different courses, so that the navigator can see at a glance what correction to apply to any course he wishes to steer.

THE BINNACLE

This is the stand in which the magnetic compass is placed on board a ship. The ship's standard compass (its main one) will usually be situated high up on the charthouse roof, as far away from any disturbing magnetic influence as possible. A second, steering compass will be mounted near the wheel for the helmsman, with perhaps a third one right aft at the hand-powered, emergency steering wheel.

Apart from supporting the compass in gimbals, the bin-

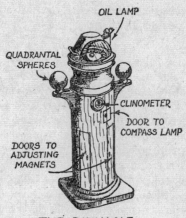

THE BINNACLE

nacle contains correcting magnets and soft-iron correctors which can be adjusted to compensate for most of the errors due to deviation.

The two round spheres mounted athwartships, one on each side of the binnacle, are soft-iron correctors which nullify the effect on the compass of non-permanent magnetism in the horizontal soft iron of the ship.

The brass top of the binnacle, chromium-plated these days, can be removed so that an azimuth mirror can be placed over the compass bowl for the purpose of taking bearings.

THE MAGNETIC COMPASS ROSE

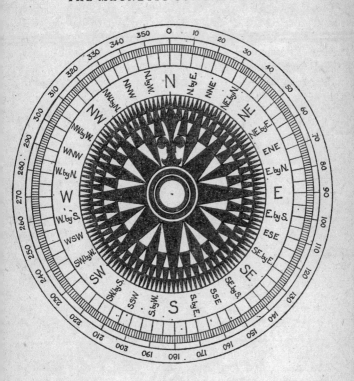

When the compass has been adjusted, a record is made of the number of magnets and their positions, and the binnacle doors are then locked.

It is the practice in big ships to check the compass every watch against the amplitude or azimuth of the sun. An amplitude is the true bearing that the sun gives when it rises or sets on the horizon. An azimuth is the true bearing of the sun in 'azimuth' (horizontal angle) when it is above the horizon.

No steel or iron object must ever be placed in the vicinity

of a binnacle containing a compass in use. The worst crime of all would be to place a magnet or another compass nearby.

SEAMANSHIP

New 'International Regulations for Preventing Collisions at Sea' were introduced on September 1st, 1965. The gist of these rules is as follows:

LIGHTS AND SHAPES

Lights shall be exhibited from sunset until sunrise.

A vessel is 'under way' when she is not at anchor, made fast to the shore, or aground.

A 'short blast', by sound, is of one second's duration.

A 'prolonged blast' is from four to six seconds' duration.

A power-driven vessel under way shall carry:

A white light on the foremast showing forward from port beam to starboard beam.

A vessel over 150 feet long shall show a second similar white light forward or abaft the first light, but the forward light must be lower than the after light.

A green light from the bow to the starboard beam.

A red light from the bow to the port beam.

A tug shall carry, in addition to the green and red side lights, two white lights facing forwards, or three if the tow exceeds 600 feet in length. (By day, a black diamond shape, where it can best be seen.)

A vessel not under command shall carry two all-round red lights or, by day, two black balls or shapes where they can best be seen.

A hampered vessel, ie, laying submarine cable, surveying, salvage, etc, and unable to get out of the way, shall show three all-round lights in a vertical line; red, white, red; or, by day, two round red shapes with a white diamond in between.

A vessel minesweeping shall carry in addition to her normal lights a green all-round light on her masthead and a second one on the side on which danger exists. By day, two black balls in lieu of green lights.

A sailing vessel under way, and any vessel being towed, shall carry the green and red side lights, and the sailing vessel may also carry a red light over a green light at the foremast head showing forward.

Small vessels which, due to bad weather or other reason, cannot carry their fixed lights, shall show a green light to starboard, and red light to port when approached by another vessel.

Power-driven vessels of less than sixty-five feet may carry

SHIPS' NAVIGATION LIGHTS

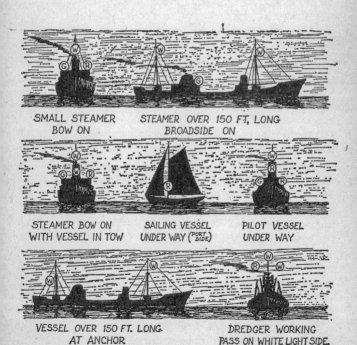

SMALL STEAMER
BOW ON

STEAMER OVER 150 FT. LONG
BROADSIDE ON

STEAMER BOW ON
WITH VESSEL IN TOW

SAILING VESSEL
UNDER WAY (PORT SIDE)

PILOT VESSEL
UNDER WAY

VESSEL OVER 150 FT. LONG.
AT ANCHOR

DREDGER WORKING
PASS ON WHITE LIGHT SIDE.

their green and red side lights in a combined lantern lower than the white forward light.

Vessels of under forty feet, under oars or sails, if they do not carry fixed side lights, shall show a green light to starboard and a red light to port in order to prevent collision.

Small rowing boats, whether under sail or oars, shall show a white light when approached by another vessel.

A power-driven pilot vessel, when under way and on duty, shall carry an all-round white light at the masthead and a similar red light beneath it, in addition to her normal lights. She may also show flare-up lights or an all-round intermittent white light. A sailing pilot vessel omits the all-round red light.

A fishing vessel engaged in trawling shall carry two all-round lights, green over white, above her side lights.

Fishing vessels, other than trawlers, show two vertical lights, but red over white.

Fishing vessels not making way through the water do not show their side lights or any stern light.

Fishing vessels over sixty-five feet show, by day, two cones one above the other with their points together, but if under sixty-five feet a fishing basket may be substituted for the cones.

Except where otherwise provided in the Rules, a vessel under way shall carry a white stern light showing from one side to the other, or shall show a white light when being overtaken, in time to prevent collision.

A vessel, when at anchor, shall show an all-round white light forward where it can best be seen. A vessel over 150 feet in length shall show a second all-round white light at the stern, but fifteen feet lower than the forward light. Between sunrise and sunset, a vessel at anchor shall carry, forward, a black ball two feet in diameter.

A vessel aground shall carry the anchor lights and the two red lights for a vessel not under command. By day, she shall show three black balls one above the other.

Any vessel on the water may, to attract attention, show a flare-up light or use a detonating or other sound signal.

Nothing in the Rules shall interfere with the operation of any special rules made by governments with respect to signal lights for ships of war, vessels sailing under convoy, or fishing vessels fishing as a fleet etc.

A vessel under sail and power shall in daylight carry, forward, a black cone with its point downwards.

SOUND SIGNALS IN FOG

A power-driven vessel of over forty feet shall be provided with a whistle for use in fog and a sailing vessel of over forty feet shall be provided with a fog horn and a bell.

A power-driven vessel when making way in fog shall give a prolonged blast at intervals of not more than two minutes. When under way but stopped in fog, she shall give two prolonged blasts.

A sailing vessel under way in fog shall, at intervals of one minute or less, give one blast when on the starboard tack, two blasts on the port tack, and three blasts when running before the wind.

A vessel at anchor in fog shall ring a bell for five seconds at minute intervals, and if over 350 feet in length, shall sound a gong in the afterpart of the vessel.

Any vessel at anchor in fog may sound one short, one long and one short blast in succession, to give warning of her position.

A hampered vessel in fog, that is under way but unable to get out of the way, shall sound at intervals of not more than one minute one prolonged blast followed by two short blasts.

A vessel under tow in fog, if manned, shall give one prolonged blast followed by three short blasts.

A vessel aground in fog shall give three distinct strokes before ringing the bell for five seconds, followed by a further three strokes.

A vessel of under forty feet, or a rowing boat, is only required to make some efficient sound signal of any sort at intervals of less than a minute.

A power-driven pilot vessel, on duty, may identify herself in fog by giving four short blasts.

Every vessel, when in fog, shall go at moderate speed, and

power-driven vessels, hearing a fog signal ahead, shall stop their engines and navigate with caution.

STEERING AND SAILING RULES

Risk of collision can be ascertained by carefully watching the compass bearing of an approaching vessel. If the bearing does not alter, risk of collision exists.

When two sailing vessels are approaching one another, one of them shall keep out of the way of the other. When each has the wind on a different side, the one with the wind on the port side shall keep out of the way of the other. When both have the wind on the same side, the vessel which is windward shall keep out of the way of the other.

When two power-driven vessels are meeting end-on, each shall alter course to starboard, leaving each other port to port.

When two power-driven vessels are crossing, the vessel which has the other on her starboard side shall keep out of the way of the other.

A power-driven vessel shall keep out of the way of a sailing vessel, but this does not give the right to a sailing vessel of hampering a power-driven vessel navigating narrow channels.

Any vessel not required to keep out of the way by the rules shall hold her course and speed, except when collision cannot be avoided by the action of one vessel alone.

Every vessel directed by the rules to keep clear of another shall avoid crossing ahead of the other.

Every power-driven vessel directed to keep clear by the Rules shall, if necessary, slacken speed, stop, or reverse her engines.

Every vessel overtaking another from abaft the beam shall keep out of the way of the overtaken vessel.

Every power-driven vessel shall keep to that side of the fairway or channel which lies on the starboard side of each vessel.

Whenever a power-driven vessel is approaching a bend in a channel, where a vessel approaching from the other direction may not be seen, she shall give one prolonged blast on her whistle within one-half mile of the bend.

Small power-driven vessels of less than sixty-five feet shall not hamper a large vessel navigating a narrow channel.

Vessels shall keep out of the way of vessels fishing, but fishing vessels must not obstruct a fairway.

In obeying the Rules, due regard shall be had to all dangers of navigation and collision and any special circumstances, including the limitations of the craft involved, which may render a departure from the Rules necessary in order to avoid immediate danger.

NOTE: Anyone going to sea in command of any vessel should make a point of studying the Regulations for Preventing Collision at Sea in detail as the above are only brief extracts from the Rules.

THE 'RULE OF THE ROAD' AT SEA

The following 'jingle', easily memorized, effectively sums up the action to be taken on meeting other ships when under way at night:

> *When upon my port is seen,*
> *A steamer's starboard light of green,*
> *There's not much for me to do,*
> *For green to port keeps clear of you.*
> *But if to my starboard, red appear,*
> *It is my duty to keep clear,*
> *To port, to starboard, back, or stop her,*
> *To act as judgement says is proper.*

And another little one:

> *When two lights you see ahead,*
> *Starboard wheel, and show your red.*

SOUND SIGNALS FOR VESSELS IN SIGHT OF ONE ANOTHER

One short blast – I am altering my course to starboard.
Two short blasts – I am altering my course to port.
Three short blasts – My engines are going astern.

Any power-driven vessel directed under the Rules to hold her course and speed, and in doubt as to whether the other vessel is taking sufficient action to prevent collision, may indicate such doubt by giving five short blasts on her whistle.

CHAPTER ELEVEN

Flag Signals and Flag Etiquette

FLAGS AND ENSIGNS

At sea, flags and ensigns are not flown to look pretty -- which they do — but to communicate a message of one sort or another.

There are several flags which ships fly when at sea, the principal one indicating the ship's nationality. This is the ensign, which she wears at the stern in a powered vessel, or at the 'peak' of the aftersail in a gaff-rigged sailing boat. With a Bermudan-rigged boat, the ensign is flown two-thirds of the way up the 'leech' of the sail.

All vessels entering or leaving a foreign port, or when at anchor there, must fly their national ensign. A British vessel of over fifty tons must fly her ensign when entering or leaving a British harbour by day or by night, and whilst in harbour, from 8 AM in summer (9 AM in winter) until sunset.

The British ensign is red with the Union Flag in the top corner. The Union Flag, commonly known as the Union Jack, is never worn at sea, except by Royalty and the Royal Navy.

The Union Flag with a white border around it, is the Pilot Jack, and this IS worn at sea, as it is the international day signal for British ships when requiring the services of a pilot in any port in the world.

The national flag of any nation, having a white border around it, is the Pilot Jack of that country.

The White Ensign is only flown by Royal yachts, the Royal Navy, and members of the Royal Yacht Squadron. The Blue Ensign is flown by special government departments, such as Customs, etc. A defaced Blue Ensign or a defaced Red Ensign can only be flown by a yacht whose owner holds a warrant from the Admiralty, and is a member of a yacht club holding a similar warrant. Also, the yacht may not wear these special ensigns unless the owner is in effective control.

It is laid down in the Merchant Shipping Act that 'if any distinctive colours except the Red Ensign . . . are hoisted upon any ship or boat belonging to a British subject without a warrant from the Admiralty, the master of the ship or boat, or the owner thereof, if on board the same, and every other person hoisting the colours . . . shall for each offence incur a fine not exceeding five hundred pounds'. This also applies to any ship or boat on inland waters – so 'watch it'.

A defaced ensign is one that includes a design on the plain 'fly' of the ensign, such as the eagle and crown on the Blue Ensign flown by members of the Royal Air Force Yacht Club.

BURGEE

This is a small triangular flag flown at the masthead of a yacht, bearing the distinguishing design and colours of a particular yacht club. It should always be worn with the ensign. The burgee is replaced by racing flags, or prize flags, when yachts are engaged in such activities.

HOUSE FLAGS

As the name implies, it is the distinguishing flag of a company or private owner, and can be of any design providing it does not infringe any Admiralty or Board of Trade regulations or any other registered design. In single-masted vessels, it would be worn on the starboard yardarm, or two-thirds of the way up the starboard main shrouds. In most two-masted vessels, it is flown at the main masthead.

INTERNATIONAL CODE FLAGS

The new International Code of Signals, 1969, has been designed so that ships and shore stations of any nationality can

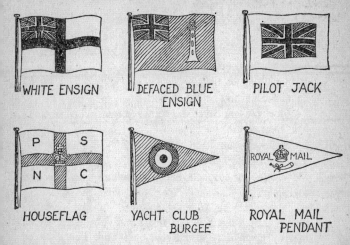

WHITE ENSIGN   DEFACED BLUE ENSIGN   PILOT JACK

HOUSEFLAG   YACHT CLUB BURGEE   ROYAL MAIL PENDANT

easily communicate with each other. Each letter of the alphabet and each numeral has its own flag, together with first, second and third substitute flags for the repetition of any letter in a group.

Each letter of the alphabet, flown by itself, has a special meaning – for instance, 'D' means 'Keep clear of me – I am manoeuvring with difficulty'.

Two-letter groups have been allotted significations next in importance, and consist mostly of distress and manoeuvring signals, together with a few general signals in constant use.

The single-letter signals can easily be memorized – and have to be by seamen:

Flag

A I have a diver down; keep well clear at slow speed.

*B I am taking in, or discharging, or carrying dangerous goods.

C Yes (affirmative or 'The significance of the previous group should be read in the affirmative').

*D Keep clear of me; I am manoeuvring with difficulty.

*E   I am altering my course to starboard.

F   I am disabled; communicate with me.

G   I require a pilot. When made by fishing vessels operating in close proximity on the fishing grounds it means: 'I am hauling nets'.

*H   I have a pilot on board.

*I   I am altering my course to port.

J   I am on fire and have dangerous cargo on board: keep well clear of me.

K   I wish to communicate with you.

L   You should stop your vessel instantly.

M   My vessel is stopped and making no way through the water.

N   No (negative or 'The significance of the previous group should be read in the negative'). This signal may be given only visually or by sound. For voice or radio transmission the signal should be 'NO'.

O   Man overboard.

P   **In harbour.** All persons should report on board as the vessel is about to proceed to sea.
     At sea. It may be used by fishing vessels to mean: 'My nets have come fast upon an obstruction'.

Q   My vessel is 'healthy' and I request free pratique.

*S   My engines are going astern.

*T   Keep clear of me; I am engaged in pair trawling.

U   You are running into danger.

V   I require assistance.

W   I require medical assistance.

X   Stop carrying out your intentions and watch for my signals.

Y   I am dragging my anchor.

Z   I require a tug. When made by fishing vessels operating in close proximity on the fishing grounds it means: 'I am shooting nets'.

Notes:

1. Signals of letters marked * when made by sound may only be made in compliance with the requirements of the International Regulations for Preventing Collisions at Sea, Rules 15 and 28.
2. Signals 'K' and 'S' have special meanings as landing signals for small boats with crews or persons in distress. (International Convention for the Safety of Life at Sea, 1960, Chapter V, Regulation 16).

Only those signals marked with an asterisk should be used with a signal lamp, using morse code.

The groups of letters carry more complicated messages but, except for a few important two-letter groups, they cannot be committed to memory and it is necessary to have a copy of Vol 1 *International Code of Signals, Visual*, published by HM Stationery Office.

Signal flags are of distinctive patterns and colours so that they can be easily interpreted under difficult conditions of visibility.

They are hoisted by signal halyards on the yardarm or crosstrees. Power-driven vessels, although they may not carry any sail, usually have a small mast for signalling purposes.

SALUTING

Saluting is normally dispensed with in confined waters. The Royal Yacht, Royal Naval ships, and ships flying their ensigns are saluted by lowering the ensign slowly halfway, leaving it dipped until the other vessel has dipped her ensign, and then hoisting it slowly again. Small launch and boat ensigns are never dipped in salute.

MOURNING

During national mourning, or on the death of the owner, a vessel wears her ensign, burgee and house flag at half-mast.

ROYAL MAIL PENDANT

Vessels carrying HM Post Office mail under contract, fly a white pendant having a red crown over a horn and the words 'Royal Mail' on it, when entering or leaving harbour.

PETROL FLAGS

Vessels carrying petrol or similar dangerous cargoes sometimes fly a square red flag with a white disc in the centre.

DRESSING SHIP

On special occasions, when in port, ships are 'dressed overall' to present a colourful rainbow pattern. International Code flags are strung together in a special order so that the different colours are distributed evenly and no particular colour predominates anywhere, and they are flown from the bows to the mastheads and back down to the stern.

If the occasion is a national one, the Red Ensign is worn at the principal masthead, but if it is only a private or local celebration, such as a regatta, the burgee retains its normal position.

FOREIGN PORTS

When any vessel is in a foreign port it is the custom, as a mark of courtesy, to fly the ensign of the country being visited from the masthead, starboard yardarm, or crosstrees.

CUSTOMS FLAG

Any vessel arriving from a foreign port is required to fly the yellow square flag 'Q', by day, or to show a red light over a white light by night. This signifies that 'my vessel is healthy and I request free pratique'. No one must board the vessel until she has been cleared by Customs officers and the yellow flag has been hauled down.

A British yacht cruising around the British coast and having 'bonded stores' aboard, ties an overhand knot in her ensign when entering port as an indication to the Customs officers. Bonded stores are those taken aboard on which Customs duty has not been paid – a privilege extended only to foreign-going vessels.

DISTRESS SIGNALS

When a vessel is in distress and requires assistance, she will fly the International Code flags 'NC', or any square flags and, above or below them, a ball, or anything resembling a ball – a round 'fend-off' or buoy would do.

Other signals might be made, such as a gun or explosive device, fired at intervals of about a minute. Red stars fired at regular short intervals; flames of any description; a smoke signal giving off orange smoke; the signal SOS ($\cdots$ — — — $\cdots$) in sound, or flashing light; a continuous sounding with any fog signal apparatus, or the slow, repeated raising and lowering of outstretched arms.

Although not a recognized signal, except in the United States, the ship's ensign flown upside down also indicates distress.

A SAILOR'S LIFE: WATCHES AND BELLS

Life at sea is divided up into 'watches' of four hours' duration, except for the 'dog watches' from 4 PM to 8 PM, when the duty lasts for only two hours.

The watches commence at 12 midnight, so the watch is changed at 4 AM, 8 AM, 12 AM and so on.

The first half-hour of the watch is indicated by the ringing of the ship's bell – 'ding'. At the end of the first hour the bell is rung twice 'ding ding' – two bells. The bell is rung in singles and couples, so that five bells would be rung as 'ding ding – ding ding – ding'.

Eight bells denotes the change of watch, except for the first 'dog watch'.

Appendices

1: THE MORSE CODE

THE ALPHABET

A	· —	J	· — — —	S	· · ·
B	— · · ·	K	— · —	T	—
C	— · — ·	L	· — · ·	U	· · —
D	— · ·	M	— —	V	· · · —
E	·	N	— ·	W	· — —
F	· · — ·	O	— — —	X	— · · —
G	— — ·	P	· — — ·	Y	— · — —
H	· · · ·	Q	— — · —	Z	— — · ·
I	· ·	R	· — ·		

NUMERALS

1	· — — — —	6	— · · · ·
2	· · — — —	7	— — · · ·
3	· · · — —	8	— — — · ·
4	· · · · —	9	— — — — ·
5	· · · · ·	0	— — — — —

2: LIFEBOAT STATIONS IN THE BRITISH ISLES

Berwick-upon-Tweed
Holy Island
North Sunderland
Boulmer
Amble
Newbiggin
Blyth
Cullercoats
Tynemouth
Sunderland
Seaham
Hartlepool
Teesmouth
Redcar
Runswick
Whitby
Scarborough
Filey
Flamborough
Bridlington
Humber
Skegness
Wells
Sheringham
Cromer – No 1
Cromer – No 2
Caister
Great Yarmouth
  (Gorleston)
Lowestoft
Aldeburgh
Walton and Frinton
Clacton-on-Sea
Southend-on-Sea
Margate
Ramsgate
Walmer
Dover
Dungeness
Hastings
Eastbourne
Newhaven
Shoreham Harbour

Selsey
Bembridge
Yarmouth (IoW)
St Helier
St Peter Port
Poole
Swanage
Weymouth
Lyme Regis
Exmouth
Torbay
Salcombe
Plymouth
Fowey
Falmouth
Coverack
The Lizard-Cadgwith
Penlee
Sennen Cove
St Mary's
St Ives
Padstow
Clovelly
Appledore
Ilfracombe
Minehead
Weston-super-Mare
Barry Dock
The Mumbles
Tenby
Angle
St David's
Fishguard
New Quay
Barmouth
Criccieth
Pwllheli
Porthdinllaen
Holyhead
Moelfre
Beaumaris
Llandudno
  (Orme's Head)

Rhyl
Hoylake
New Brighton
Lytham-St Anne's
Blackpool
Fleetwood
Barrow
Workington
Ramsey
Douglas
Port St Mary
Port Erin
Peel
Kirkcudbright
Portpatrick
Girvan
Troon
Campbeltown
Islay
Mallaig
Barra Island
Stornoway (Lewis)
Longhope
Stromness
Stronsay
Lerwick
Aith
Thurso
Wick
Cromarty
Buckie
Whitehills
Fraserburgh
Peterhead
Aberdeen
Gourdon
Montrose
Arbroath
Broughty Ferry
  (Dundee)
Anstruther
Dunbar
St Abbs

Eyesmouth
Portrush
Donaghadee
Goughey
Newcastle
Clogher Head
Howth
Dun Laoghaire

Wicklow
Arklow
Rosslare Harbour
Kilmore
Dunmore East
Helvick Head
    (Dungarvan Bay)
Youghal

Ballycotton
Courtmacsherry
    Harbour
Baltimore
Valentia
Fenit (Tralee Bay)
Galway Bay
Arranmore

Glossary of Nautical Terms

The following definitions are reproduced from the Glossary in *Reed's Nautical Almanac* by courtesy of the publishers, Thomas Reed Publications Limited. Page numbers refer to more detailed descriptions appearing in the text.

ABAFT	Towards the stern.
ABEAM	At right-angles to the line of the keel.
ABOUT	To go about, to change tack.
ADRIFT	Broken away – no longer fast to the shore or ground.
AFT	Towards the stern of the vessel.
ALOFT	Above the decks, up the masts or rigging.
AMIDSHIPS	Midway between stem and stern. 'Midships' is order to put rudder fore and aft.
ANCHOR BUOY	Small buoy attached to anchor. Serves to indicate position of anchor and provides means of recovery if cable should break, or have to be slipped.
ASTERN	Behind the vessel.
ATHWART	From side to side.
AVAST	To stop, to hold fast, eg, 'avast heaving'.
AWASH	A vessel, wreck, or shoal so low that water constantly washes over.
AWEIGH	Term to indicate that the anchor has broken out of the ground.
BACK	Wind shifting anti-clockwise.
BACKSTAY	Standing rigging from a masthead leading aft to take the strain of the mast.
BAGGYWRINKLE	Rope chafing gear fastened to stays, to save chafe when in contact with sails.
BALE	To remove water from a small boat by baler.
BALLAST	Iron, lead or stone placed in bottom of a ship to increase her stability.
BAR	A shoal in the approach to a harbour. (*page* 65)
BARE POLES	When a vessel is under way with no sails set.
BATTEN DOWN	To fasten all hatches, skylights, openings before proceeding to sea.

BATTENS	Thin pieces of wood or plastic set into the sail to preserve the shape.
BEACON	Aid to navigation, lighted or unlighted, set on the shore or rocks. (*page* 18)
BEAM	(*a*) Extreme width of a vessel. (*b*) Athwartships timber on which the deck is laid.
BEAM ENDS	When a vessel is forced by wind or sea on to her side.
BEARING	The direction of an object at sea expressed in compass notation.
BEAR UP	To put the helm up, ie, keep further away from the wind.
BEATING	Sailing towards the direction of the wind by tacking.
BECKET	Small rope circle, a simple eye.
BELAY	To make a rope fast to a belaying pin or cleat.
BELAYING PIN	Metal or wood pin (but movable) set in a rail to belay ropes to. (*page* 108)
BELLS	Used in all vessels when anchored in fog; also the sailor's clock. (*page* 139)
BERMUDAN RIG	A triangular sail hoisted on a tall mast. (*page* 78)
BIGHT	Any part of a rope between the ends; also a curve or cove on a coastline.
BILGES	Bottom of vessel where water collects.
BINNACLE	The box which houses the mariner's compass. (*page* 124)
BITTS	Pair of wooden or iron heads vertical on deck with crosspiece for fastening cables. (*page* 107)
BOBSTAY	A stay for the bowsprit to prevent it lifting; led from bowsprit end to stem at waterline.
BOLLARD	Heavy short post on a quay or deck to secure ships' mooring lines to. (*pages* 102, 106)
BOOM	A spar for many purposes, such as to stretch out the foot of a sheet block aft.
BOOMKIN (BUMKIN)	Small spar fastened to the stern projecting aft to carry the fore and aft sail.
BOOT-TOPPING	A band of paint at the waterline between 'wind and water'.
BOWER	Main anchor carried forward in a vessel.
BOW	Forward part of a vessel.
BOWSPRIT	Heavy spar from deck leading forward from stem head to set head sails. (*page* 100)
BREAST-HOOK	Horizontal knee set across inside the bows to strengthen them.
BRING UP	To stop, as to come to anchor.
BROACH TO	To come up to the wind and get broadside into the trough of the sea.
BROAD REACH	With the wind on the quarter.

BULKHEADS	Partitions fore and aft or athwartships, forming separate compartments.
BULL'S EYE	A hardwood round thimble scored to take the eye of a rope.
BULWARKS	A vessel's topsides that extend above the deck. (*page* 109)
BUNK	A built-in bed aboard ship.
BUOY	A floating beacon with distinguishing name, shape, colour or light. (*page* 24)
BUOY, MOORING	The buoy that indicates the ground tackle for a vessel to moor to. (*pages* 30, 31)
BURGEE	Swallow tail flag indicating the yacht club the vessel's owner belongs to. (*pages* 99, 134)
BY THE LEE	When running under sail, if the wind blows over the same side as the mainsail.
CABLE	(*a*) Nautical measurement 100 fathoms (200 yards), one-tenth of a nautical mile. (*b*) The chain (or rope) that is attached to the anchor. (*pages* 57, 99)
CAPSTAN	A vertical cylindrical machine for veering or hoisting the anchor chain. (*pages* 20, 105)
CAREEN	To heel a vessel over on one side by tackles, to work on her bottom.
CARRY AWAY	To break off.
CARRY WAY	To continue to move through the water.
CARVEL	Edge to edge planking for a vessel's hull. (*page* 76)
CAULK	To fill the side or deck seams with oakum or cotton to prevent leaking. (*page* 76)
CENTREBOARD	A wood or metal plate lowered through the sailing boat's bottom to prevent leeway. (*page* 74)
CHAFE	Chafing gear, canvas, or the like wound round ropes and spars to prevent wear by rubbing.
CHAIN PLATES	Metal strips fastened outside the hull to take the rigging strain. (*page* 101)
CHART	A map showing the sea and coastline details. (*page* 120)
CHOCK-A-BLOCK	When two blocks of a tackle come together – also 'two blocks'.
CLAW OFF	Working a vessel to windward off a lee shore.
CLEAT	A two-pronged device for making fast ropes. (*page* 106)
CLEW	The corner of the sail where the leech meets the foot.
CLINKER	Planking when one edge overlaps the other lower plank. (*page* 76)
CLOSE-HAULED	Sailing close to the wind.

COCKPIT | A well in a sailing boat from which it is steered. (*page* 72)

COMPANION | Ladder in a ship.

CON, TO | To give orders to the helmsman in narrow waters.

COUNTER | The overhanging portion of a stern. (*page* 85)

COURSE | The direction a vessel steers in. (*pages* 119, 120)

CRADLE | The frame erected round and under a vessel to support her out of the water.

CRINGLE | Rope round a thimble, worked into a sail clew.

CROWN | (*a*) Where the arms of an anchor meet the shank. (*b*) The knot when the strands of a rope are interlocked to make a backsplice. (*page* 103)

CRUTCH | (*a*) Metal fitting dropped into gunwale of a small boat, often called rowlocks. (*b*) A stanchion with half round upper end to support the boom (also Gallows).

DAVITS | Iron crane for hoisting, lowering and holding boats in position in larger vessels. (*pages* 41, 103)

DEAD RECKONING | The position found by calculation from course steered and distance run.

DEADEYES | Round hardwood blocks with holes for lanyards to set up lower rigging. (*page* 101)

DEADWEIGHT | Total weight of vessel's carrying capacity in tons. (*page* 54)

DEADLIGHTS | Round hinged plates fastened inside glass portholes in bad weather.

DEADWOOD | Heavy timbers at bow and stern just above the keel. (*page* 72)

DECK | Flooring of a vessel. Given different names in larger vessels.

DECKHEAD | Underside of a deck. The roof of a ship's cabin.

DEEP | (*a*) Unmarked soundings of the lead line. (*b*) Deep water channel between shoals. (*page* 116)

DOLPHIN | A built pile structure for mooring in harbour.

DOLPHIN STRIKER | A spar underneath the bowsprit to spread the martingale.

DOWNHAUL | Rope or tackle used to haul down sail or yard.

DOWN HELM | Order to helmsman to put tiller *away* from the wind; *up helm* is towards wind.

DOWSE | (*a*) To extinguish a light. (*b*) Lower sail or spar quickly.

DRAFT MARKS | Figures fastened or painted on bow and stern; lower edge is exact foot. (*page* 114)

DRAUGHT | The depth of water occupied by a vessel at any time. (Also Draft.)

EBB	The period when the tide falls or flows from the land.
ENSIGN	The flag, always carried at the stern, that denotes a vessel's nationality. (*page* 133)
FAIRLEAD	A channel for leading a rope over an obstruction to avoid friction. (*pages* 61, 109)
FAIRWAY	Shipping channel, normally the centre of an approach channel.
FAIR WIND	Wind abaft the beam.
FALL	Normally the hauling part of a purchase by which, eg, boat is hoisted.
FATHOM	Nautical measurement of depth of six feet. (*page* 116)
FEND-OFF	To prevent touching when coming alongside; to keep off.
FENDER	Soft rubber or other material to prevent chafe between vessels, or vessel and pier. (*pages* 43, 61)
FID	Wooden marline spike. Also pin in hole at foot or end of spar or mast.
FIDDLE	Wooden top with divisions fitted to saloon table in rough weather.
FILL	When a wind stretches the sheets and 'fills' the sail.
FISH	To fish a spar is to lash another spar to it for strengthening purposes.
FLAKE	Complete round turn when coiling down a rope clear for running.
FLARE	The overhang of a vessel's bow; also a light signal by pilots and fishermen.
FLAT ABACK	With the wind well on the wrong side of the sail.
FLATTEN IN	To haul in the sheets of a fore and aft sail.
FLY	Length of a flag – horizontal measurement.
FLYING	The outer headsail whose luff is not hanked to a forestay.
FOOT	The lower edge of a sail.
FOOTROPE	A wire rope hanging below a yard for men to stand on.
FORE	The foremast and the name applied to its sails and rigging.
FORE AND AFT	In line with the keel – lengthways of the ship.
FOREFOOT	Rounded part of the stem below the water.
FORWARD	Towards the bow, ie, 'Forward of the beam' between 45 degrees and 90 degrees from the bow.
FOUL	Opposite to clear, as 'foul berth', 'foul anchor', 'foul bottom', 'foul hawse'.
FREE	Not close hauled.

FREEBOARD | The distance from the waterline to the deck outboard edge.

FRESHEN | (a) To renew, as 'freshen the nip' of a rope hawser. (b) Wind freshens when increasing.

FULL | Said of a sail when drawing well.

FULL AND BYE | Close-hauled but with the sails well filled.

FURL | Gathering in sails and securing with gaskets to its spar.

GAFF | The spar to which the head of a fore-and-aft sail is bent. (page 79)

GALLEY | The kitchen of a ship of any size.

GALLOWS | Frame of wood or metal with rounded top for supporting the boom.

GANGPLANK | Temporary bridge between ship and shore.

GATHER WAY | To begin to make headway.

GEAR | Widely used term for equipment, fittings, spars, ropes and canvas.

GIMBALS | Two concentric rings to hold the compass or stove horizontal at all times. (pages 46, 94, 124)

GO ABOUT | To tack.

GOOSE-NECK | A metal fitting for securing a boom to a mast. Allows swing and topping.

GOOSE-WINGED | When running and the aftermast sail is out on the side opposite to the foresail.

GREEN SEA | The term used when solid water is shipped aboard.

GRIPES | Holding lines to secure a ship's boat when swung out.

GROMMET | A rope circle or brass parts used as sail or hammock eyelets.

GROUND | (a) A ship touching bottom is said to ground. (b) Ground swell is the long coastal swell.

GUNTER | A sliding gunter rig is when the gaff is hoisted vertically, reducing the necessity for a tall mast.

GUNWALE | The heavy top rail of a boat.

GUY | A rope or wire used to steady a boat, derrick or spar.

GYBE | To allow a fore-and-aft sail to swing from one side to the other when running.

HAIL | To call from or to a vessel. Also a vessel hails from her home port.

HALF-MAST | A flag hoisted halfway as a mark of respect for the dead. (page 138)

HALYARDS (or HALLIARDS) | Ropes or tackles used to hoist sails or flags. (pages 99, 105, 106)

HAND	A crew member. To furl a sail, to hand (haul in) the patent log.
HANDY BILLY	A small tackle.
HANKS	Strong clip hooks which attach headsails to the mast stays.
HARD	A place, often specially constructed, for beaching small vessels.
HAUL	To pull; the wind when it changes is said also to haul aft or forward.
HAWSE	The distance from the stern to vertically over the anchor; with two anchors down and no turns a vessel rides to a clear hawse, should the chains be crossed or have turns she has a foul hawse.
HAWSE PIPES	Pipes leading down through the bows through which the anchor cables are led.
HAWSER	A heavy rope used for mooring, kedging, warping, towing or as a temporary anchor warp. (*page* 98)
HEADS	Toilets in a ship.
HEAVE	To throw, also the movements, ie, rise and fall of a ship at sea.
HEAVE AWAY	To commence hauling, on rope or anchor chain.
HEAVE SHORT	To heave in the anchor chain till nearly vertical, ready to sail.
HEAVE THE LEAD	To take soundings. (*page* 115)
HEAVE TO	To stop; by sail or engine action to so reduce speed that when head into wind a vessel has as little forward motion as possible. Vessel is then 'hove to'.
HEAVING LINE	Light line, knotted on end to throw ashore when berthing as a messenger for a larger mooring line. A seaman will take pride in a correct throw. (*page* 100)
HEEL	A list from the upright; the foot of a mast.
HELM	The tiller or wheel; the helmsman is he who steers a vessel.
HITCH	To make a rope fast to a spar or stay, but not to another rope.
HOIST	To raise aloft; the height of a flag at the staff.
HOLDING GROUND	The type of bottom for anchor, ie, good or bad holding ground.
HORSE	An iron bar parallel to the deck, running athwartship for a sail sheet to travel.
HOUNDS BAND	A band around the top of the mast with securing eyes for attaching stays. (*page* 100)
HOUSE FLAG	The ship or boat owner's personal flag. (*page* 134)
HULL	The body of a boat, but not including the interior fittings above or below deck.

INBOARD	Towards midships.
INSHORE	Towards the shore.
IRISH PENNANT	A loose end hanging anywhere from aloft.
IRONS	A vessel is in irons when caught head to wind and unable to pay off on either tack.
JACKSTAY	An iron rod, secured to a yard for bending sails to.
JACK STAFF	Small staff in the bows from which the jack is flown.
JACOB'S LADDER	A rope ladder with wooden steps.
JAWS	The forked end of a boom or gaff that partly go round a mast.
JIB	The triangular sail set as the forward headsail. (*page* 79)
JURY	After losing mast or rudder an expedient makeshift rig to get the vessel to safety.
KEDGE	A lightweight anchor for kedging or warping.
KEDGING	Moving a vessel by hauling on a kedge warp fast to a kedge anchor.
KEEL	The heavy backbone of any vessel, running fore and aft, on which the vessel sits when grounded. (*page* 72)
KEELSON	A secondary keel lying fore and aft above the main keel (*page* 72)
KING SPOKE	The spoke of the steering wheel which is upright when the wheel is amidships.
KINK	A twist in the lay of a rope which prevents free running.
KNOT	One nautical mile per hour. (*page* 113)
LACING	The long line that secures the sail to a spar through eyelets.
LAID UP	Vessel out of use, generally tied to a buoy or pier or in a yard.
LANDFALL	The point on a coast that a vessel first sights coming in from the sea.
LANYARD	(*a*) The ropes that reeve through the deadeyes for setting up the rigging. (*b*) In practice it is a small rope for making anything fast.
LAY (verb)	To go, ie, lay aft or lay aloft, lay to (ie, heave to) lay up, lay a course.
LAY (noun)	The twisting of strands in a rope. (*page* 98)
LAZY	An extra, such as a lazy painter, ie, an extra painter.
LEECH	The after side of a fore-and-aft sail, and the outer sides of a square sail.
LEAD	The lead weight at the end of the lead line used to find depth of water. (*page* 115)

LEE SIDE	The side away from the wind direction.
LEE-BOARDS	Heavy boards like a centreboard but lowered on the lee side of a shallow draught vessel to prevent lee-way. Also the boards on the outside of a bunk to prevent the occupant falling out.
LEEWARD (loo'ard)	Towards the sheltered side.
LEEWAY	The sideways drift of a vessel from her course to leeward, due to wind pressure. (*page* 119)
LEG	A tack, eg, when going to windward a vessel may make a long leg and a short leg.
LEGS	Heavy wooden timbers whose heads bolt to the outside of a small vessel for supporting a vessel upright when put ashore.
LET DRAW	To allow a vessel to fill on the correct tack.
LET FLY	Let go sheets in an emergency.
LET GO	Order to drop the anchor into the water.
LIFEBUOY	Circular ring, of cork, metal or other buoyant material.
LIFELINE	Lines stretched fore and aft along the deck in heavy weather for crew to hold on to.
LIFT	(*a*) Fog is said to lift when it disperses. (*b*) A rope or wire to support a spar as topping lift.
LINE	Small rope, but always called line at sea, ie, log line, heaving line, etc.
LIST	When a vessel heels through having greater weight on one side.
LOG	An instrument for recording the distance run. (*page* 112)
LOG BOOK	The record of events on board a ship, especially navigational.
LOOM	The reflection on the clouds when the light is still below the horizon; also an oar handle. (*page* 10)
LUBBER LINE	Line on the inside of a compass bowl indicating the ship's head.
LUFF	To keep closer to the wind; forward edge of a sail.
LUG	A small boat rig, eg, dipping lug and balanced lug. (*page* 78)
MAKE, TO	To attain, ie, to *make* harbour. *Make* fast is to secure. Tides that *make* increase. To *make* eight bells is to strike the four double strokes at end of watch. *Make* sail is to set sail. *Make* water is to leak.
MAN	To man is to provide hands to do work as *man* the boat, *man* the capstan; *man* the falls; *man* the yards is to stand men from yardarms to mast as a salute.

MARLINE SPIKE   Pointed steel tool for opening strands of rope when splicing.

MARRY   To bring two ropes together by holding or seizing temporarily.

MASTER   The captain of a merchant vessel.

MASTS   Vertical spars set in to a vessel to carry sails or derricks, etc.

MIDSHIPS   Order to the helmsman to centralize the rudder.

MISS STAYS   To stay up in the wind when tacking.

MOOR   To moor is to lie with two anchors down. Vessels are said to be moored to a jetty when well made fast with several mooring lines.

MOORINGS   Permanent anchors and chains laid in shallow water with a smaller vertical chain made fast to the heavy ground chain; floated by a buoy which is pulled aboard to reach the light chain to secure the ship to. (*page* 30)

MONKEY ISLAND   Compass platform atop wheelhouse.

MOUSE, TO   Taking several turns with light line across the mouth of a hook to prevent the rope becoming unhooked.

NEAP TIDES   When the tide does not rise or fall much, when the moon is in quadrature. (*page* 44)

NEAPED   Of a grounded ship when the tide does not rise high enough to float her.

OFFING   To seaward.

OLD MAN   The usual crew name for the master of a merchant vessel; also a horizontal roller on a pedestal to lead ropes to a winch barrel.

PARREL   A rope or iron for securing a yard or iron to the mast.

PAY OUT   To ease a chain or rope.

PITCHING   A ship's movement in a seaway in a fore-and-aft direction.

POOPED   A term to indicate that a heavy sea has come inboard over the stern causing damage.

PORT   The left-hand side of a ship looking forward.

PORT TACK   To sail with the wind on the port side before the beam.

RAKE   The inclination of the mast in the fore-and-aft line from the vertical.

RATLINES   Horizontal ropes as steps affixed to the shrouds to facilitate climbing. (*page* 100)

REACH	The courses of a sailing vessel between being sailed close hauled and running.
REEFING	To reduce sail area by taking in at the reefing points.
RUN	A day's run is the total distance covered in twenty-four hours.
RUNNING RIGGING	That rigging which is not standing, eg, halyards, gantlings, purchases, etc.
SAGGED	When the extremities of a ship have bent upwards.
SCANTLINGS	The dimensions of a ship's timbers.
SCUTTLES	Round holes in the ship's side for ventilation and light.
SEIZED	To lash. Also refers to metal being jammed solid.
SHEER	The rise of a ship's deck towards the bow or stern from amidships.
SHEER STRAKE	The upper line of plating or planking on the hull.
SHELLBACK	Hardened experienced seaman.
SHIPSHAPE	In a seamanlike manner.
SHORTEN SAIL	To take in or reduce sail.
SLANT OF WIND	A favourable wind.
SOUND	To measure the depth of water by lead line or electronic means. (*pages* 117, 118)
SPLICE THE MAIN BRACE	A special issue of rum.
SPRING	A mooring rope. A back spring is a mooring rope led from forward aft or from aft forward. (*page* 99)
SPRING TIDES	Tides when the moon is full or new, that is when the range of the tide is greatest. (*page* 44)
STAND ON	Maintain course.
STARBOARD	The right-hand side of a ship facing forward.
STARBOARD TACK	With the wind on the starboard side forward of the beam.
STOVE IN	Broken in.
TACKLE	A purchase of ropes and blocks. (*pages* 41, 103, 108, 110)
TAKE UP	To tighten.
TIGHT	Not leaking.
TILLER	Lever for turning the rudder. (*page* 72)
TOGGLE	A piece of wood for making fast an eye on its own part.
TOP HAMPER	Weight carried on deck or aloft which at times may prove an encumbrance.
TRICK	A period at the wheel.
TRIM	Refers to how the vessel is floating.

TUMBLE HOME	Where a ship's sides are inclined inwards above the waterline.
TWO BLOCKS	When a purchase can go no farther as the blocks are together.
UNDER WAY	When a vessel is moving and not made fast to the ground.
UP AND DOWN	Vertical, a term used in anchor work.
VANG	A guy for steadying a gaff.
VEER	To ease out a cable. A clockwise shift of the wind.
WAIST	The middle part of the upper deck.
WARPING	Moving a vessel by means of a hawser.
WEATHER SIDE	The side upon which the wind is blowing.
WEATHER TIDE	Where the tide is making against the wind.
WEAR SHIP	Turning a ship around before the wind, keeping the sails full (the opposite to tacking a square-rigged vessel).
WEIGH	To lift the anchor off the ground.
YARD	A spar suspended from a mast, to spread the sails.
YAW	When the ship's head is swung by the action of the waves.
YOUNG FLOOD	The first movements in a flood tide.

Index

THE MOST SOUGHT AFTER SERIES IN THE '70s

These superb David & Charles titles are now available in PAN, for connoisseurs, enthusiasts, tourists and everyone looking for a deeper appreciation of Britain than can be found in routine guide books.

BRITISH STEAM SINCE 1900   W. A. Tuplin   45p
An engrossing review of British locomotive development – 'Intensely readable' – COUNTRY LIFE. Illustrated.

LNER STEAM   O. S. Nock   50p
A masterly account with superb photographs showing every aspect of steam locomotive design and operation on the LNER. Illustrated.

OLD DEVON   W. G. Hoskins   45p
'As perfect an account of the social, agricultural and industrial grassroots as one could hope to find' – THE FIELD. Illustrated.

INTRODUCTION TO INN SIGNS
Eric R. Delderfield   35p
This beautifully illustrated and fascinating guide will delight everyone who loves the British pub. Illustrated.

THE CANAL AGE   Charles Hadfield   50p
A delightful look at the waterways of Britain, Europe and North America from 1760 to 1850. Illustrated.

BUYING ANTIQUES   A. W. Coysh and J. King   45p
An invaluable guide to buying antiques for pleasure or profit. 'Packed with useful information' – QUEEN MAGAZINE. Illustrated.

RAILWAY ADVENTURE   L. T. C. Rolt   35p
The remarkable story of the Talyllyn Railway from inception to the days when a band of local enthusiasts took over its running. Illustrated.